WHEN
THE NIGHT
COMES FALLING

ALSO BY HOWARD BLUM

NONFICTION

The Spy Who Knew Too Much
Night of the Assassins
In the Enemy's House
The Last Goodnight
Dark Invasion
The Floor of Heaven
American Lightning
The Eve of Destruction
The Brigade
The Gold of Exodus
Gangland
Out There
I Pledge Allegiance . . .
Wanted!

FICTION

Wishful Thinking

WHEN
THE NIGHT
COMES FALLING

A Requiem for the
Idaho Student Murders

HOWARD BLUM

HARPER

An Imprint of HarperCollins*Publishers*

HarperCollins books may be purchased for educational, business, or sales promotional use. For information, please email the Special Markets Department at SPsales@harpercollins.com.

FIRST EDITION

Designed by Nancy Singer

Library of Congress Cataloging-in-Publication Data has been applied for.

ISBN 978-0-06-334928-5

24 25 26 27 28 LBC 5 4 3 2 1

For Graydon Carter, Alessandra Stanley, and Ash Carter,
who pointed the way, and kept me on course.
With gratitude and friendship

"A voice was heard in Ramah,
weeping and loud lamentation,
Rachel weeping for her children;
she refused to be comforted, because they are no more."

—Jeremiah 31:15

CONTENTS

A NOTE TO THE READER

"People talk."

That insight had been passed on to me by Sydney Schanberg, the hard-charging metro editor of the *New York Times*, back when I was a cub reporter. I'd been trying to chase down the intricacies of a complex story spilling across the South Bronx that involved narcotics, cops, voodoo, and, at final count, thirty-eight murders—and I had come up empty-handed. Frustrated, I was *this* close to giving up. "Keep knocking on doors. Keep going around," Syd counseled. "You'll be surprised what people will eventually tell you. People talk."

So I kept at it. And after eight months or so of me putting in my time, Syd proved right. People had slowly opened up, and I had my story; in fact, it turned out to be a six-part series.

When I set off to a wintry Idaho to report on the perplexing murders of four college students, I tried to keep Syd's advice front and center in my mind. But my confidence flagged after a stern judge issued a gag order that, for all valuable purposes, prohibited anyone with firsthand knowledge of the events from speaking with the press. Then, another obstacle, there were some people who, in spite of the court's ruling, made it clear that they'd be willing to share what they knew, but only for a price. It was tempting, yet I ultimately decided that sort of transaction didn't sit right with me.

I plowed on. In the course of a hectic and exhausting year, I made many trips to Idaho, Washington State, and Pennsylvania. I knocked on doors. Took people to dinner. Had coffee in hospitable living rooms. Downed Rolling Rocks in roadhouse bars. And I worked the phone incessantly. Another boon: I had made some friends in law enforcement over my years working an investigative reporter's beat, and I called in those chips, too. Then, as the case moved forward, from the arrest warrant to the grand jury indictment to the motions the defense and the prosecution filed as they prepared for trial, a small mountain of legal documents, many filled with fascinating revelations, began to pile up. These all allowed me to get behind the scenes and into the minds of many of the characters in this story.

More often than not, my sources insisted that I could not reveal their names; either the consequences of violating the gag order weighed heavy on their minds, or they feared professional retaliation from their law-enforcement bosses. Also, it should be noted that individuals included in this narrative, whether as a result of the gag order or their wanting financial remuneration, or for their own personal reasons, refused to be interviewed. Nevertheless, by drawing on their public statements as well as detailed, revelatory conversations I had with their friends, relatives, business associates, and in reviewing their social media postings, I was able to share what they were thinking and feeling. I could make them come alive on the page without their having agreed to an interview. I was, therefore, able to write this account of the Idaho student murders—a true story about people caught up in horrific events—with a firsthand insight, authority, and accuracy. And with some surprising revelations. A brief chapter-by-chapter Note on Sources follows at the end of this volume.

But for now, it's simply sufficient to know that Syd had once again been right: people talk.

PART I

MICHAEL'S STORY

Michael Kohberger (forefront) and his son Bryan head home for the holidays. A cross-country journey filled with secrets. *Credit: Indiana State Police*

ONE

Suppose you wanted to kill someone.

That would be easy. There are lots of ways.

But suppose you wanted to kill four people. All in the same house. All within moments of one another. And you chose to use a knife.

That could help eliminate the noise. But it would require skill, strength, and patience. Murder is hard work, especially if people fight back.

Then there's the really big hurdle: you want to get away with it. You're determined to stab four people living in a single home in the still of the night and then disappear without leaving a clue to your identity. Now, that's a more difficult challenge.

But you did it! The perfect crime.

Michael Kohberger woke up early to check on the weather, but instead learned about the shooting.

It was not long after dawn on December 15, 2022, the big Kansas sky still gray and solemn, and his night's sleep had been fitful. He felt out of sorts, a complaint he'd continually make as the days ticked down to Christmas, but he blamed his unease on all the travel. It was an explanation that made good sense; in the hectic span of little more than a week, Michael, a graying sixty-seven-year-old who had already started to feel the aches and pains of his senior years, had been shuffling through a disruptive flutter of time zones as he made his way back and forth across nearly the entire width of the country.

Just five days earlier he'd flown off in harsh sunshine from Philadelphia to Seattle, then caught a twin-engine Embraer E170 jet for the one-hour-or-so shuttle flight into a dark, frigid Pullman (Washington)-Moscow (Idaho) Regional Airport. There was a long walk from the plane to the squat, single-story terminal, and the evening cold hit him like a punch. It was a lonely, desolate outpost, and particularly so when gripped by the long shadows of the northwest winter; the runway had been bulldozed out of the vast, dunelike hills of the Idaho Palouse, and the matchbox-sized airport was the only sign of civilization in a rutted, lunar-like landscape that spread into the distance toward a foreboding wall of amber mountains.

But Bryan, his twenty-eight-year-old son, had, as promised, been there to meet him, and from the airport it was just a twelve-minute drive (if the roads weren't slick with frost) to Bryan's apartment across the state line in Pullman, Washington. To his doting father's pride, Bryan had just finished his first semester as a PhD candidate in criminal justice at Washington State University, an accomplishment that, to any objective eye, was an academic success story. Bryan had been a mediocre student at a hardscrabble high school in blue-collar Pocono Valley, Pennsylvania, where Michael had been the maintenance man. Upon graduation, he stumbled, without any real interest, into a local community college. But then, as if by magic, once he started his college coursework, a long-submerged burst of ambition and focus rose up. He did well enough to transfer to nearby DeSales University, an institution firmly Jesuit and rigorous, where, after earning a BA in psychology, he switched to criminal justice and received his master's. Then, with the support and encouragement of his DeSales professors, he was accepted into

Washington State University's nationally acclaimed doctoral program. It was the same prestigious university where Michael's sister-in-law, his older brother Clement's wife, had impressed the family by getting a degree in psychology. For Michael, who had never gone to college, this was an astonishment. He had grown up in the rough-and-tumble city streets on the industrial periphery of the Brooklyn Navy Yard, where his father had also been a maintenance man. The fact that his son was well on his way to a doctorate—"Dr. Bryan Christopher Kohberger" was how he was already referring to him in a conversation with a mechanic at a local garage just days before he flew to Seattle—was a cause for immense pride. Things he could only have dreamed of would be accomplished by his son. And it was a future that seemed even more remarkable when Michael allowed himself to look back at the painful tumult of Bryan's teenage years.

"Complicated"—that was the tactful euphemism that Maryann, his wife for nearly four decades, would finally settle on when talking about their son. But Maryann was, Michael knew, always more gentle, always more outwardly caring to their two older daughters and young Bryan than he was. And after all, patience was part of her job; she was a diligent paraprofessional working with special-needs pupils in the Pennsylvania school district where he was the janitor. Yet for Michael, he'd frankly acknowledge to relatives, all he had gone through with the boy had thrown him for a loop. It was not just that he had been unprepared to raise such a troubled child, but the cascade of problems were of a sort that was more than he could fathom. He rejoiced that it was all in the past.

Or was it? For when pressed, an exasperated Michael would share with his two grown daughters, one a psychologist, the other an aspiring (and "aspiring" was very much the operative adjective) actress, that "there's really no telling what Bryan might do next." And that was arguably why he had decided to make the tedious and exhausting trip out to Pullman, Washington, and then, not much more than twenty-four hours later, turn around as if on a dime to make the even more monotonous and draining car ride back across the country with Bryan as his son returned to the family home in Albrightsville, Pennsylvania, for the monthlong winter break. He wanted to show Bryan that he cared. He wanted to make up for all the hostility that had erupted from both their corners during the trying years. And, not least, he wanted to see what was up with his son. The past five months had been the longest period that Bryan, in all his twenty-eight years, had been away from home, and his father wanted to gauge how the boy had handled things. He wanted to explore close up which version of himself Bryan, who had shown himself to be a master of disguise, was now presenting to the world. Four long days trapped shoulder to shoulder in the nearly claustrophobic confines of a Hyundai Elantra as they made the twenty-five-hundred-mile journey promised the sort of proximity that could be filled with revelations.

Yet right from the start, Michael felt that something was up. They had started to argue, and the sheer scale and intensity of his son's objections threw Michael for a loop. He felt ambushed by the force of Bryan's anger.

The issue under heated debate was the route home. In the weeks before heading off from Pennsylvania, Michael had done his homework. Sitting at the computer console that was perched as usual on the kitchen table, he did a series of Google searches. The quickest, most logical drive, he discovered, was pretty much a straight line. They should plow east across the country along I-90. He had shared this itinerary with his son in a phone call around Thanksgiving, and Bryan had breezily agreed with the reasoning.

Only now that they were about to drive off from his son's spartan single-room apartment in Pullman, Washington, Bryan had kicked that plan to the wayside. Instead, he insisted that they buttonhook south through Colorado, where they'd then pick up I-70. It was an itinerary that made little sense to Michael. For one thing, Colorado in mid-December was snow country; there was no telling when a storm might suddenly come blowing down from the Rockies. And if weather came in, it'd be rough going in Bryan's seven-year-old Hyundai Elantra; without four-wheel drive, you'd be slipping and sliding all over the road. And for another, it was a longer route. Even if they got lucky and didn't cross paths with a snowstorm, it'd still add days to their journey.

But the more Michael tried to explain, the more Bryan dug in. It was a volatile dialectic that Michael had suffered through too many times in the past. So he surrendered. "You're the boss," he later told people he'd said, deciding to defuse things. Because, as he'd later share with the family and they'd pass on to friends, he had started seeing the sort of warning signs he knew only too well. Bryan, the unflinching authority. Bryan, the deep thinker who always knew better. When the boy got into this hardheaded, know-it-all mood, Michael's go-to response was to back off. To go with the flow. And after all, confrontations had never sat well with him.

But that didn't mean Michael had given up worrying about the weather. Sure, they had made it through Colorado without encountering any snowfall, but an early winter storm swooping across the Great Plains would be no less of a catastrophe. So now that he was fully awake, he asked Bryan if he had checked his phone for the latest forecast.

Without a word, according to the account his family shared with relatives, Bryan handed him the device. Michael read:

"WSU Alert Pullman: SWAT team is actively working on the south side of campus. Shelter in place until further notice."

And all at once, everything that had been nagging at him since his reunion with his son, all the emotions that he had not dared to name, rose to the surface in a sudden fear.

THE DETAILS, AS HE WOULD harvest them that morning from the radio news and the Internet, were sparse. But in time Michael would get a fuller picture, and it served to exacerbate his concerns.

At around 8:00 the previous evening, at the off-campus Coffee

House Apartments—an ugly three-story complex offering utilitarian student housing that was only a stone's throw from the similarly stark development where Bryan lived and Michael had just camped out for an uncomfortable night—a rifle-toting resident had threatened to kill his two roommates.

The Whitman County Regional SWAT Team came in heavy. An eighteen-ton armored mine-resistant ambush protected (MRAP, in military parlance) vehicle had lumbered down snow-dusted Latah Street in the starry night and positioned itself directly opposite the building where the two students were held hostage. Painted in big black letters on the tanklike vehicle's khaki-colored hood were the initials JRD. This was a tribute to Deputy Justin DeRosier, a former member of the team. At the same time, it also was a cautionary reminder: DeRosier had been shot dead while checking out nothing more ominous than a poorly parked motor home. The moral: you never know what's waiting for you out there.

"Two Two Two!" The command from the team's tactical leader screeched over the walkie-talkie, and immediately about a dozen heavily armed cops began blocking off the perimeter, keeping returning students and passersby well clear of the complex. At the same time, officers began hurriedly escorting bewildered students out of the building into the wintry night; a makeshift shelter had been hastily set up in Beasley Coliseum, a university athletic arena.

By now a negotiator had gotten through to the apartment on a phone line. The gunman identified himself as Brent Kopacka and he was talking a mile a minute and not much that he said made any sense. All the negotiator could make out was panic, rage, and chaos. The cursory bio the sheriff's office had pulled together on Kopacka pushed the threat level up another notch: He was a thirty-six-year-old former US Army paratrooper who had served in Afghanistan. He returned with a Purple Heart, a traumatic brain injury, and a tormenting case of PTSD he'd been trying to shake off for the past sixteen years. The last time the local cops had encountered Kopacka, he had been belligerently arguing with a voice rising up from under a manhole cover. The resigned mood among the front-line SWAT officers held that things could very quickly go from bad to worse, and the team had better move in while there was still hope of getting the hostages out alive.

But as the SWAT leader was poised to issue the "go" order, the two hostages walked out of the building. Kopacka had told them to get the hell out before he changed his mind. And just like that the team exhaled. The cops fell back, taking cover behind the bulk of the MRAP or crouching low in the heavy shadows cast by the wall of interconnected apartment buildings. They'd wait and let the negotiator talk the guy down.

Then the shooting started. From the second-floor window, Kopacka began firing a long-barreled weapon toward the MRAP. When a bullet found its mark, the ping off the armor plating echoed sharply through the taut night. And Kopacka was ranting. Angry, largely incoherent messages boomed out; things had gone beyond reason.

The order came to open fire, and now the tree-lined college town streets crackled with the echoes of battle. The firefight went on with sporadic intensity for a while, but before dawn, a decision was made. Seven hours was enough; things had to be resolved before students headed to class.

"Take him out!" the SWAT commander ordered at about 4:00 a.m.

Had there been any thought about firing tear gas through the apartment's window? A volley of stun grenades? Or simply playing things long, letting the decorated army veteran continue firing until he ran out of either ammunition or rage? The answers to those questions remain hidden in the Palouse Area Law Enforcement Critical Investigation Response Team report that was finally filed six months later and immediately stamped CONFIDENTIAL. All that is a public certainty is that in the instant after a two-handled metal battering ram smashed open the plywood apartment door, a SWAT team sergeant stormed in and shot the rifle-toting Brent Kopacka dead.

———

THAT WAS, AT LEAST IN its broad, unsettling strokes, the story that Michael had pieced together from news reports as he drove across Kansas in the brisk morning with his son. And it made his blood run cold.

What was wrong with people out there in the northwest? he had wondered angrily, according to a conversation family members had subsequently shared with friends. Another violent death—the fifth!—in a Palouse college town.

Less than a month earlier, in November, four University of Idaho college students had been found dead, hacked to death in their off-campus house. No one understood why or who was responsible.

This was a broken place, Michael decided. Maybe it had something to do with the mountains, the higher altitudes, he speculated, according to the family conversations that were passed on. Or maybe it was just the west. When his parents separated, his four brothers and his mother had headed out from Brooklyn to Las Vegas. But Michael had stayed behind with his father, and even when he visited them, he had found the desert beyond the city lights a haunted place. "Spooky" was how he had always described it. And the northwest, he had grown convinced, was no better. Demons seemed to be haunting the adjacent college towns of Pullman, Washington, and Moscow, Idaho.

Michael worried for his son, and couldn't wait to get him home, away from all this. Delays were a constant anxiety. As they drove east through Kansas toward Indiana, he was on the lookout for the first slow flakes of falling snow. Perhaps that was why he never noticed the small, single-engine fixed-wing Cessna 182 that was constantly above them, shadowing their journey home like a watchful hawk waiting for the moment when it would swoop down to strike.

TWO

Yet, this was not Michael's first cross-country road trip with his son. At the tail end of July, barely five months earlier, he had been riding shotgun in the passenger seat of the same white Hyundai as they made their determined way west from the Poconos to the Pullman, Washington, campus. Back then, the air-conditioning in the tight little car had been cranked up high and the worry had been that the darkening summer skies would erupt in fearsome thunderstorms; driving in the wake of mammoth eighteen-wheelers sluicing down the highway would be a risky business. And that time, too, Michael had found little that was pleasant in the prospect of such a disruptive, whirlwind journey; the plan was that he'd be flying out of Seattle and heading back to Philly only days after he arrived.

Nevertheless, last summer, he had decided it was a necessity to make the arduous trip alongside his son. To an outsider, such attention might seem overly vigilant, even controlling. After all, Bryan was closing in on thirty, a fully grown man by any standard. He would be a teaching assistant at WSU; he'd be lecturing and grading papers, a doctoral candidate, not some immature undergrad. However, Michael, according to several knowledgeable accounts, was resolute: he would not be deterred from traveling with Bryan. And he had a head full of long-nurtured reasons for such careful paternal attention.

Duty, the always-beating heart of a father's love, fueled one strand of his thinking. His wife, who had a gentle, maternal soul, might as well have been speaking for both of them when she posted on Reddit on the eve of Bryan's departure. "My son will be in Pullman in the eastern part of the state quite close to the Idaho border!" she announced with mawkish concern. "He knows absolutely NO ONE and we have no family there! I worry about him being lonely . . . !" Michael, who knew a few things about loneliness—his mother, when he was still a teenager, had hightailed it to Las Vegas, leaving him behind in Brooklyn to be raised by a father who had little time for child-rearing—didn't want Bryan to despair as he set out to get acclimated to life on his own in an unfamiliar corner of the country. A father's familiar presence, he believed, would help make the transition a bit easier. Last thing he wanted, given Bryan's often unsettled moods, was for his son to feel the pressure of standing at one of life's crossroads all by himself.

And in equal measure, it might be argued, guilt had been a motivator, too. Michael wanted to make up for all he had put his son through. After all, it was one sort of handicap to raise three children on a janitor's salary. A janitor whose finances were such a catastrophe that he had to file for bankruptcy only a year after his son had been born. And it was still another sort of free-falling descent into abject poverty when, just as Bryan turned sixteen, a besieged Michael felt he had no choice but to take refuge for a second time under the federal bankruptcy statutes; this go-around, when he emptied his pockets, all he could find for the court was $15 in cash and $49.77 in a savings account. It was not a nest egg that could bankroll the boy's college education, or, for that matter, even purchase a pair of Air Jordans for his birthday.

Trying to get by with only pennies in the bank was the sort of familial drama that, Michael couldn't help but feel with regret, might have laid the toxic groundwork for his son's turbulent adolescence. And Bryan sure had had a rough go of things. That weighed heavy on Michael. Yet while Maryann would try to console rather than judge their son, relatives would say, Michael's reaction was more harsh. Exasperated, he'd lecture Bryan that the boy was his own worst enemy. "Bryan," he'd admonish, "you need to get your act together." He'd rail that the boy's problems were all of his own making. Nevertheless, there was one thing for which Michael knew he alone was to blame.

And even after all the years that had passed, he couldn't shake off his guilt: he had turned Bryan into the cops.

It was an act of desperation, and yet that didn't diminish its sting for both the father and the son. Michael's father had a record for stealing a car on a trip to Miami, and now Michael had made sure his son would be branded with a similar scar, grandson like grandfather. But at the time, Michael had just not seen any other way. His nineteen-year-old boy was out of control. The arrest, he'd wanted to believe, would be a wake-up call. It would be for Bryan's own good.

BRYAN SAW THINGS DIFFERENTLY. BUT then again, it was not his time for understanding. Nothing made sense, and nothing was all that he could feel. He had forged a kinship with despair, and it mattered little to him that his behavior—combative one day, detached the next—took a toll on his family. Something beyond his control was playing with his head. "Mind fizzle," he called it.

Looking for a remedy, or even just a diagnosis, as Bryan turned fifteen, he found solace in an online community composed of people who believed they were suffering from visual snow. This was a rare, but painfully real, chronic neurological condition that played havoc with one's visual perception of things. To the afflicted, the world was viewed through a glass darkly. It was like looking at a television screen and the picture was always fluttering, the images obscured by amorphous grayish waves and scattered, flickering dots. But was it a disease? Or was it a psychological condition? Doctors, according to the sparse literature, threw up their hands in frustrated confusion. They just didn't know. And what can't be diagnosed was even more difficult to treat.

But there was no disputing that it sure took its toll on teenage Bryan. If his online posts were a reliable guide, visual snow had buried him under an avalanche of unhappiness. Day after downhearted day, he went on the Web to shout out his calls from the wild.

I feel like an organic sack of meat with no self-worth . . . I am starting to view everyone as this.

Everything I have ever done makes no sense. How did things get this way?

I always feel as if I am not there, completely depersonalized . . . Constant thoughts of suicide. Crazy thoughts. Delusions of grandeur . . . poor self-image.

It is like I have severe brain damage. I am stuck in the depths of my mind, where I have to constantly battle my demons.

In this high-voltage state, Bryan couldn't decide whether his family was to blame for the maelstrom that was pulling him under, or if they were offering a life raft that could float him off to a safe place. In the end, though, he judged that he had sunk too deep to be saved.

As my family hugs and celebrates, I am stuck in this void of nothing, feeling completely no emotion, feeling nothing. I feel dirty, like there is dirt inside of my head. . . .

But there was still room in this void for regret.

I think about my father, what a good man he is, how I treat him like dirt because I have this condition, and I can't take it. . . .

Everything in his life added up to less than zero, and Bryan was resigned to this grim mathematics. It was even, he apparently decided, liberating. He could do "whatever I want with little remorse." He was beyond rules, beyond laws.

And he was angry. He went on SoundCloud to howl out a rap song that seemed to have been composed during a blizzard of visual snow: "You are not my equal / You are evil but I'm devil."

Which, Michael grieved, made him the devil's father.

THEN BRYAN FOUND A WAY to free himself from his pain—heroin.

At the time, as the second decade of the twenty-first century dawned, drugs were running wild in Monroe County, PA, and their trafficking was an open secret. It was easy to score; every teenager, or so it seemed, either had a connection or knew someone who did. In rural Pleasant Valley High School, where Bryan was enrolled, it was as much a part of the gloom as the dirty, bullet-gray snow that lay piled high for much of the winter on the shoulders of the narrow, twisting county roads or the junkyards littered with the rusting carcasses of abandoned cars. The local statistics on overdoses and opioid use were a heartache. Too many kids who had gone to Pleasant Valley didn't make it out of their early twenties alive, and their classmates spent a lot of time at the funerals of friends. For Bryan, it was Jeremy Sabo, the happy-go-lucky kid with the mop of wild hair who lived two houses down.

Sabo had started his official descent with guilty pleas to a DUI and a misdemeanor possession of drug paraphernalia and, undeterred, then spiraled further. He soon pleaded guilty for a misdemeanor: possession of a controlled substance, and after serving a year's probation, he celebrated his freedom only to end up dying, the coroner's report ruled, of an accidental overdose. And it was Sabo who, friends say, got Bryan to try smack.

But it was Ashley Flugel, a bouncy, free-spirited high school classmate, who helped Bryan become a junkie. They would routinely score from a dealer who did a brisk business selling stamped glassine packets of heroin from his perch adjacent to a local bowling alley, and then they'd rush off to shoot up. Bloody track marks, classmates recall with dismay, ran up their arms.

Over time, Ashley had developed a serious habit, and it wasn't long before it all caught up with her. She was facing an intimidating array of drug charges, including a felony count of intent to distribute a controlled substance, but before her court appearance, she overdosed.

Bryan, meanwhile, was trying to find a way out. In February 2014, now enrolled in community college, he went to rehab. But it was a half-hearted gesture, and it didn't stick. It wasn't long before he was back using. And his habit had become increasingly expensive. Desperate, he stole his sister Melissa's new iPhone. He had to pay a kid he knew $20 to drive him to the local mall, where there was a kiosk that bought used electronics, no questions asked, and he sold the $400 device for $200 cash. Then he went off to score.

It didn't take his family long to figure out what had happened to Melissa's phone.

Michael had had enough. Either Bryan return the phone to his sister, or he would report the theft to the police.

"Don't do anything stupid," Bryan warned.

But Michael was in no mood to be intimidated. The cops came and Bryan was arrested. True, it was more theater than retribution; as a first-time offender, Bryan entered a Monroe County program (Accelerated Rehabilitative Disposition was the official name) that required no jail time, just a year's probation. After a year had passed, his record was expunged. And his heroin addiction was also history.

AS HE WAS CLOSE TO turning seventeen, a new version of Bryan began to take shape. Determined to be a different man, he made up his fierce mind and lost, friends would estimate, well over one hundred pounds of fat. Chubby, full-cheeked Bryan was history, and a new, sleeker Bryan with chiseled cheekbones, thick, wavy hair, electric eyes, and a swaggering smile had emerged.

And he was determined to keep this new look. With a convert's fanaticism, the ex-junkie went full vegan. He not only wouldn't ingest any animal products, but he also refused to be served food that might have been cooked in pans that had once prepared meat. His body had become a temple, and now he was also setting out to turn it into a fortress. He started heading out for long runs over the countryside, taking boxing classes, lifting weights, and doing rigorous sets of push-ups. He was dreaming of turning fat into sinewy muscle. Where he once had a belly, he wanted to sculpt a six-pack.

But in the transformative process, Bryan encountered an unexpected and damn embarrassing problem. He had lost so much weight that the excess, inelastic skin now hung over his lower abdomen and genitals like the bouncing flap on an envelope. It was gross; certainly not the sort of appendage a hunky guy wanted. So Bryan went under the knife. It was expensive, but he had medical insurance. When Bryan was wheeled out of the operating room, the surgeon had performed both a panniculectomy and an abdominoplasty; his abdomen and his lower belly had been expertly contoured to create the same flat, rock-hard torso he had admired on the other fighters in his boxing class.

Bryan was at last starting to feel he was becoming the man he was meant to be. He had always been intelligent, possessing the sort of mind that liked to bore down deep into things, but he just didn't have the confidence to exhibit his acuity. But now it was as if he was trying to make up for all the time he had held his peace. He'd hold forth, his students would later complain, "like he was the smartest guy in the room." And in Pennsylvania, his old friends—a ragtag collection of the sort of outcasts who, like Bryan himself, had been bullied all through middle school—were bristling, too. To hear them tell it, they felt betrayed. "Bryan's acting all high and mighty," one groused. "I liked him better when he was chubby."

But Bryan, apparently, had no regrets. When he met up with his old crowd, he'd act superior, quick on the draw with a put-down, or he'd wrestle someone into a headlock and then prance around in a victory dance like he was the champion of the world. Bryan wanted them to realize that he had moved on.

But to where? He certainly hadn't become the player he apparently believed would come hand in hand with his new sleek look. The girls who had bullied the fat kid in middle school still didn't want to date the new, reinvented Bryan. Women, Dominique Clark, a classmate would recall, found him "odd," "a creep." "If he liked or was interested in a girl, and she wasn't, he just didn't understand why or just didn't accept her saying no."

But he kept trying. A Tinder date with Hayley, a coed from Penn State Hazleton while Bryan was at Northampton Community, ended up with the frazzled young woman locking herself in the bathroom pretending to vomit just so he'd leave her dorm room. The desperate ploy worked, and Bryan, the would-be Romeo, vanished passively into the night. But an hour later, he had the last word. He texted Hayley to let her know that he thought she had "good birthing hips." That was the clincher. Hayley summarily blocked him from her contacts.

Such was Bryan's romantic life.

BUT NOW HE COULD MAKE a fresh start. As he arrived with his dad in a sunny Pullman, Washington, in the first week of August 2022, the campus was already a hive of activity although the new semester had not yet officially begun. Everywhere Bryan looked, a parade of sun-kissed coeds scurried about in the seemingly prescribed uniform of tight cutoffs and artfully cropped tops that exposed tanned midriffs. Who could have blamed Bryan if he felt the excitement that comes with the promise of a new adventure?

Only Michael, a concerned father, had his doubts. He worried that Bryan, or at least the unbalanced and complicated rendition that he knew, would keep to himself. And so when he headed out for a stroll and spotted Bryan's new next-door neighbor in the apartment complex parking lot, he hurried toward him.

Michael had briefly met Christian Martinez the previous day, when Bryan and he were lugging the cardboard cartons up the two flights to apartment G-201. Martinez, though, was not easy to forget. He was big and burly like a linebacker, and an intricate tattoo tapestry ran up his neck.

"Bryan's shy," Michael explained. "Has a hard time making friends."

Martinez, who was by nature polite, listened sympathetically.

"Maybe you could look out for him?" Michael suggested.

THREE

Christian Martinez was a high-spirited, very sociable fellow, and he and his wife, Holly, had a large circle of friends. It was an older group since Martinez had served in the military and had a few years on most WSU undergraduates. Martinez also pulled together a lot of people with family backgrounds similar to his, students and recent grads with roots in the Latino and Hispanic community. And they were a fun-loving crowd, always up for something. When they weren't off hiking in the nearby mountains, they'd fly to Vegas for a weekend or simply head out for some beers in downtown Pullman, hitting the Emporium or Stubblefields.

And so as the new semester edged closer, one of Martinez's buddies, Zach Cartwright, reached out to him with the promise of a final summer bash. Cartwright was a man of many parts. He had a recent doctorate in food science, but in addition to his research job at a local food processing company as part of a team devising an ingenious procedure to extract moisture from crops, he made time to moonlight as a yoga instructor and a DJ. On Sunday, he eagerly explained, he had a gig DJing at an afternoon pool party at The Grove, an off-campus housing complex over in Moscow. Should be wild. Tell all your friends, he urged.

All my friends? As Martinez began spreading the news, the chance encounter a few days earlier with his new neighbor's father came to mind. The old man had no valid claim on him, and his son certainly wasn't a friend, barely an acquaintance, in fact. But Martinez decided it'd be a kindness. And it wasn't as if he'd have to babysit the guy; a pool party on a sunbaked August afternoon, one of the last blowouts before classes would begin, was certain to attract a crowd. It'd be just the sort of gathering where even a newcomer could make friends.

Martinez texted Bryan the details, including the Southview Avenue address over in Moscow.

"Thanks! I have to run and get trunks," Bryan texted in reply.

FOR THE LOCALS, PARTICULARLY THE old-timers, the nineteen or so miles between the Washington State campus in Pullman and the University of Idaho just over the Washington state line in Moscow, Idaho, was known as "the Loser's Walk." The name was a bit of nostalgia, a throwback to the sixty-year span (ending in 1968) when the two schools had a fierce football rivalry. Tradition had it that when the final second had ticked off to end the fourth quarter, the students from the defeated school would file out of the stadium and set out on "the Loser's Walk" back to campus, their heads presumably hanging mournfully low.

But there was nothing hangdog in Bryan's mood that August afternoon when he set out on pretty much that identical route between the two campuses. He zipped down the two-lane 270 East in his Hyundai for the quick twelve-minute trip to Moscow.

It was Bryan's first visit to Moscow—many more would come in the months ahead—and the town's name must have been a puzzlement. It had only a tangential connection to the magisterial Russian capital, and an exceedingly thin one even at that. Back in the 1870s, according to the most popular theory, one of the valley's founding fathers discovered the fledgling community needed an official name before the US Postal Service would deliver its mail. He had been born near Moscow, Pennsylvania, and then had spent some years in Moscow, Iowa, and so he decided a name that had already proven satisfactory might as well be trotted out again. And after all the years the townsfolk were still quick to drive home the point that there's no connection to the Russian city; with no attempt at irony, they never missed an opportunity to inform visitors that their town's name was pronounced to rhyme with Costco.

But no matter how you said it, Moscow had always been a pretty place. In the spring, the valley sparkled with bright waves of violet wild camas plants. Then in summer, the fields of amber wheat came in, only to grow more resplendent when the deepening shades of autumn took hold. And at the same time, on the mountains on the edge of town, a glorious and extravagant display broke out. But soon enough, the snow blew in and buried everything as far as the eye could see in a pristine white cloak.

It was easy to understand why generation after generation of adventurers had decided to stop here. First came the restless pioneers and prospectors who had headed off to follow in the footsteps of Lewis and Clark. Then there were the enterprising homesteaders who were carried along by the rolling wheels of wagon trains and the federal promise of 160-acre tracts of vacant land under the Homestead Act. And finally came the ambitious entrepreneurs who headed west in big, hulking locomotives, puffs of steam blowing across the ancient trail where the Nez Perce tribe had galloped on their spotted Appaloosas. They all came, and swiftly decided there was no reason to go any farther than this splendid little valley.

A little more than a century and a half since its founding, there was still a brashness and a frontier wildness to Moscow, despite its having now swelled to twenty-five thousand inhabitants. The quaint veneer, however, disguised something untamed, savage, and reckless. And it never took much to turn it all loose. Down deep, pretty Moscow was pretty poison.

And so sure, Moscow was a university town. But while it was a good place to be a student, it was an even better place to party. The

University of Idaho came into being after President Abraham Lincoln, in the midst of the Civil War, signed the Land Grant Act. This law gave states the right to sell off vast tracts of land as long as the proceeds would be used to endow colleges where students could receive "agricultural and mechanical" training. Boise, according to the perhaps-apocryphal story recounted with glee in several state histories, had originally been designated by the legislature as the site for the new institution of higher learning. But the practical Boise city fathers argued that they'd rather be home to the new state penitentiary, a more certain boon to the local economy. And so by default, in 1889, the University of Idaho convened its first class in Moscow.

Things didn't get off to an auspicious start. Forty students assembled for the entrance exam, and none passed. The dismayed university president decided to run the institution as a prep school until he could get the student body up to college-level speed. These days, however, the University of Idaho spreads out over 800 well-landscaped acres and is home to about 8,800 undergrads. And standards have been ratcheted up considerably from the days of the school's ill-prepared inaugural class. Professors will tell you that their top students are "as good as any you'll find in the Ivy League." "But," they also quickly add with a candor shaped by frustrating experience, "the rest leave a lot to be desired." Nearly three-quarters of those who apply are accepted, and that sort of laissez-faire selectivity helps shape a student body that seems more diligent about putting in time in the Student Rec Center (famous for its state-of-the-art climbing wall) than the dreary library building that rises up like an oppressive concrete block monolith on Rayburn Street. And the school officials seem pretty complacent about their priorities, too. On the day when Bryan made his way to Moscow, a long yellow banner had been scrolled across the approach to the august Administration Building: #1 BEST VALUE IN THE WEST, it boasted, as if advertising one of the motels that lined nearby Pullman Road.

And while national surveys buried the U of I pretty far down the list when it came to academics, time after time it ranked as "the best party school in the state." Central to all the good times on and off campus was the school's deep commitment to Greek life. There were at last count a total of thirty-four fraternities and sororities tied to the school, with about a quarter of the student body—2,100 kids!—affiliated. And, sure, the frats and the sororities, as they drum earnestly into their pledges, have an impressive inventory of high-minded aims like building lifelong friendships and doing good work in the community. But take a stroll down Greek Row on a Saturday night, and the ear-popping noise will signal that there's one hell of a party going on. That kind of clamorous spirit ran deep in Moscow. For decades, after all, the town's best-known address had been 304 West A Street, the site of its most stylish brothel.

Then there was the misconception that a little town like this, with its oh-so-quaint Main Street and coffeehouses and ice-cream parlors, was a bastion of law and order. Yet back in 1945, Carol Ryrie Brink, who had grown up in Moscow, had seen enough to write that "the quick, wild urge to hurt and kill" was inveterate to the town. And she'd known this simmering danger firsthand. Her grandfather, a doctor who had been one of Moscow's founding fathers, had been shot dead for no apparent reason in 1901 by a deranged local.

More recently, in 1969, Janice Foiles, an eighteen-year-old coed, had been working behind the counter at the Tip Top Cafe late on a frigidly cold December night when her head was smashed to pieces with a claw hammer. It was a murder that was never solved. The same disquieting strangeness, too, surrounded the still-unsolved disappearance a decade later of another pretty young woman, Gayla Schaper. Just twenty-eight, she had gone out to feed the horses in the corral on the farm she shared with her husband one summer afternoon and was never seen again. The only clue after all the years remains a bizarre note, the letters cut from magazines, that she'd received days before she vanished: *You have sold out to Satan.*

Then there was the patch every local cop wears on the shoulder of their uniform. It depicts a clock tower set to 1:49. That was the badge number of Officer Lee Newbill, who was killed in 2007 when another wild gunman went racing around the town on a shooting spree after killing his wife and a church sexton, finally blowing his own skull to bloody pieces with his assault rifle.

Little Moscow, the locals grumble to one another in hushed voices, had its share of drug trafficking, too. In fact, the rising statistics on drug arrests detailed in the annual police reports made it clear that narcotics was a growth business in town.

There was also, residents were beginning to worry, another reason for concern. A Moscow police detective lieutenant had been assigned to the four-county taskforce formed to wade into the dirty waters of pedophilia. To his astonishment, he made close to a dozen arrests, and the taskforce had a backlog of over 2,200 cases in the area it considered worth digging in to.

Still, Moscow had always been a God-fearing, churchy town, and today there were more than two dozen Christian congregations. On Sunday morning, the collective chiming of the church bells rose up in a loud swell. The largest congregation, about two thousand strong and growing, however, was Christ Church. Yet the Kirkers, as the parishioners call themselves as a sign of their allegiance to Mother Kirk, an old Scottish name for the Reform Church, were in many ways a political movement as much as a religious one. Doug Wilson, their shrewd, articulate—fire-and-brimstone one moment, a measured intellectual the next—pastor and all-around mastermind, has made it clear that he has far-reaching ambitions. He wants to turn Moscow into a theocracy, "a Christian town." Walk down Main Street, and it's as if the battle lines have been literally drawn. On one side of the street is the Kirker empire: a café, a bookstore, a K–12 school, a college, and a publishing house. On the other side are the places frequented by everyone else. But the Kirkers have high hopes of increasing both their flock and their domain. They have ties to two real estate offices in town that are set on attracting the sort of zealots who are fed up with woke America and the nosy, interfering deep state.

"If you put God back in Idaho, then God will always protect Idaho" is the selling pitch. And Moscow, if the Kirkers have their way, will be the capital of the Redoubt, as the new, fiercely conservative American frontier has been christened.

Only the Kirkers' path to godliness and political power, as many seething people in town see it, had been paved with a lot of truly troublesome missteps. There was the former Christ Church deacon who was sentenced to two years in prison for possession of child pornography; the member who was found guilty of "injury to a child" because of his relationship with a fourteen-year-old girl; another who was convicted of sex offenses involving children; and in addition, there were the dozen women who went public to allege that they had been sexually assaulted by members of the church.

"No ifs, ands, or buts," a local lawyer predicted with a combative resignation, "there's a civil war getting ready to erupt in the streets of Moscow."

Such, then, were the fault lines that lay hidden beneath the outwardly pleasing little town that Bryan entered for the first time on that broiling hot August afternoon. It was a moment when he still had no awareness of the town's troubled history. Or the seething forces roiling around the Palouse. Or that it would not be long before the very mention of his name would be synonymous in Moscow with a previously unimagined evil.

FOUR

———

Perched at the crest of a small hill south of Main Street, The Grove was not, as the lyrical name suggested, a leafy copse, but rather a newish assembly of dull-colored three-story buildings. The structures spread out nearly end to end over the incline and provided, the developer's promotional brochure boasted, "first-class off-campus student housing."

It was a very popular address despite the narrow, prison-cell-like rooms fitted with desks finished in a plastic veneer meant to look like wood. It wasn't the accommodations, though, that had students opting out of dorms and frat houses to move in. The real attraction was that The Grove was one big party house. It offered up all the glittering toys that could stoke a good time: a gargantuan, shimmering blue pool; a beach volleyball court complete with sand; a barbecue setup that could grill franks and burgers for a hungover army of revelers; and, not least, a wide, parabolic-shaped deck that crawled around the pool, leaving plenty of room for mingling, dancing, and rows of coolers stocked with beer and Trulys.

Bryan parked in front of the Community Club building, people would recall, and by the time he arrived, maybe 4:00-ish, the music was already blasting. He had worn his newly purchased swim trunks under his jeans, and now he quickly stripped down in his Hyundai. Following the noise, he made his way to the pool.

Cartwright, the food science PhD, now calling himself "DJ Grape Vinyl" (it wouldn't be long, though, before he settled on the professional name "Catalyst," making sure to spell it out using triangles instead of the *a*s) manned the turntable. Bad Bunny wailed from the speakers, imploring, "Party! Party! Party!" Chicken and steak were being grilled to make tacos. There was wine, beer, and tequila. There must have been a hundred or more college kids on the deck. Bryan in his new swimsuit, ghostly pale but still looking good, bulked up, with a mop of brown curls, perched on a step at the shallow end of the pool. He was taking it all in, and his large blue eyes gave out an air of angelic perplexity.

Grabbing a seat next to Bryan was Basseth Salamjohn, a laid-back, darkly handsome off-and-on WSU undergraduate who was part of the crowd that ran with Martinez and Cartwright. The two started talking, and Salamjohn quickly decided there was something odd about Bryan's intensity. "The dude would talk chin up, straight into my face," he'd recall. "We were just shooting the shit, but he was definitely one serious dude. Nice enough, though." After a while, Salamjohn stood up and went off to dance.

So Bryan, perhaps not wanting to be left sitting alone on the pool steps like some loser, headed over to talk to the DJ. Cartwright was an imposing figure with a jet-black man bun, and he stood with a martial erectness over the turntable as he orchestrated the festivities. The time had come, his instincts told him, to take things higher, to let the music swell. He needed to focus. But he was by breeding and nature polite, so when the guy approached, Cartwright was friendly. He looked a bit lost, Cartwright decided.

Bryan started asking about the speakers. He had lots of questions, technical stuff. At first Cartwright did his best to answer; in truth, he had a nerdy streak, too, when it came to electronics, and he was proud of his knowledge. But the conversation quickly grew grating. "He had this way about him," the DJ would remember. "You know those people who don't understand personal space? He was one of them. He'd get real close. It was off-putting." Finally, Cartwright told his new acquaintance, "I'm DJing, man. I'll catch you later."

So Bryan returned to the shallow end of the pool, and before too long Salamjohn joined him, too. And he watched what happened next with a growing curiosity.

Without a word to him, Bryan abruptly jumped up and approached a girl in a black thong bikini with pink hair and an intricate tattoo running up her left thigh. There was only a brief conversation before Bryan asked her for her phone number. And he got it.

Next, to Salamjohn's further fascination, Bryan, as if a man on a mission, focused on the pink-haired woman's friend. She was also in a black two-piece. He asked her for her number, too. And he got it.

Dude's a player, Salamjohn marveled. *Got the digits! Who'da thought it?* But before he could congratulate the conquering hero, Bryan did an abrupt about-face. Just as things were picking up, he left the party.

The music was loud in Bryan's ears as he drove down the hill from the complex, heading straight past the Moscow Police headquarters on the way back to Pullman. Things, he undoubtedly felt, were taking on a brighter look.

And there was a footnote to the day's events that only many months later would provoke interest and speculation. Bryan never telephoned either of the two women. Perhaps he had lost interest. Or maybe he had only wanted to establish that he could get a spark from a pretty woman. After all, in middle school the girls had mocked him, laughed at the overweight kid. When he boldly sat down next to one of the good-looking ones in the lunchroom, they'd tell him to get lost, and an embarrassed Bryan would slink over to a table filled with his loser friends, people he secretly detested. It might very well have been he simply lacked the will—or was it confidence?—to take the next step. Maybe he felt he'd always be an outsider, someone destined to be on the periphery of the good times others would be having. All that was certain was that in the aftermath of the pool party, both women received several hang-up calls, and it wasn't until much, much later that they put a possible name to the annoying caller.

FIVE

_____

Meanwhile, on that mid-December morning nearly five months later, when father and son were making their way back home for the holidays, Bryan drove with a focused silence. The new day was startlingly bright, puffy white clouds were high in the big Midwestern sky, and Michael, he'd later share with a friend, had grown convinced that all his fears about a snowstorm had been unnecessary. He still was reflecting, though, on the horror of a SWAT team shoot-out in an off-campus neighborhood not far from where his son lived. Yet when he attempted to engage Bryan to see what he made of it all, for all his questions he had not gotten an answer worth a penny. But he had long ago grown accustomed to his son's moods. One moment the boy would be rageful, the next unapproachable, as if locked in some inner world. Soon the small car was filled with a companionable silence.

Bryan spoke up at last. There was a Thai restaurant he had found on the Web, he announced. Outside Indianapolis. They could stop there for lunch.

Sounded like a plan, Michael agreed. At first, Bryan's strict commitment to a vegan diet had left him mystified, but after all the years spent grappling with his son's many difficulties, Michael's temperament had grown more open to anything that kept him centered. And, he had to admit, maybe it was working. Gone were the truly awful days when he had to worry about whether Bryan would be found lying in a Stroudsburg alleyway with a needle in his arm. All the bewildering talk about visual snow was history, too. Heading off the interstate to hunt down a Thai restaurant rather than pulling into the next roadside McDonald's was a small inconvenience when measured against the miracle of his son's transformation.

They had turned down the heat in the car because, despite the chill outside, the high morning sun reflecting off the windshield glass was keeping things warm. Michael absently watched the passing trucks. It was an easy drive; the highway was flat and the traffic steady; they were making good time.

And as they started crossing through Hancock County, Indiana, Bryan spoke up. Only now there was a hesitancy, and Michael knew that was a warning. The one thing about Bryan, he'd tell people, was, "That boy knows his own mind. No beating 'round the bush. He'd let you know what he was thinking."

"I got a problem," Bryan finally announced.

All at once, Michael braced himself.

His apprehension eased as Bryan revealed that he was having some trouble at school. Yet for his son, it was as if a fuse had been set off. A taut-faced Bryan, Michael would tell people, ranted that a few spoiled brats in his classes were really to blame for the entire misunderstanding. They had complained that he was too demanding, too tough a grader. And, incredibly, the department's professors were siding with the malcontents. The university had no commitment to "intellectual honesty," Bryan charged, and it was at this point, Michael later confessed, that he started to have a difficult time following where things were going. Intellectual honesty? What the hell did that mean? More college mumbo-jumbo, he swiftly decided.

Truth be told, Michael would come to concede, from the start he had wondered why his son had thought it necessary to enroll in a school all the way on the other side of the country to study, of all things, criminology. What was that all about? Did Bryan need a PhD to become a cop? Was that where all this would be leading?

When Michael had first shared his misgivings last spring after his son had received the email announcing his acceptance into the WSU doctoral program in criminal justice, Bryan had gotten huffy. He was setting off on a career that was a lot more important than scribbling traffic summonses, he had barked. He'd be accomplishing the sort of things that the police could never dream of doing. He'd be studying, he said loftily, "the criminal mind." He'd be "a scientist exploring why criminals do what they do."

The indignant response told Michael it would be wiser if he kept his peace; he didn't want to start something. Still, Michael felt that you didn't need to be a scientist to solve what made the criminal mind tick. He had crossed paths with his fair share of hoods growing up by the Brooklyn waterfront. He had uncles who had gotten pinched for gambling. He had a brother, one of a set of twins, who had been charged with grand larceny and receiving stolen goods, but had gotten off with probation and fines. Hell, his own father had stolen a car. He had seen enough to convince himself that, without ever once cracking a book, he had a pretty good understanding of the criminal mind. And it all came down to this: people broke the law because it was the easiest way to get something they wanted.

And, he'd say, you want an explanation for why psychos do what they do? Why people kill? To Michael's mind, that was pretty simple, too: it was just the way they were. You can't change those sorts, or expect to understand them. That's what he had told Maryann, friends would share, when she had gone to all the trouble of getting a poem Melissa, his daughter, had written into the *Pocono Record* after the horror of another school shooting, this one in Uvalde, Texas. "Small hands and feet / buried six feet deep," Melissa had rhymed. And his wife had added an earnest postscript: "We must consider the children before the gun." But Michael just shrugged off their heartfelt sentiments. It wasn't that he didn't care. He worked all day in a school; how could he not feel aggrieved, he'd say, over the deaths of innocent school kids? But he also was of a mind that was resigned to all the madness. Nothing, he had made clear to his wife, would be rectified one iota by poems. Or, for that matter, professors trying to use big words to make sense of things. Or degrees in criminology.

Still, if this was all there was to Bryan's problem, he was relieved. Because the one thing he knew was that his boy was damn smart. "Has his mother's brains, thank God," Michael would tell people. So as Bryan continued to lay out in increasingly bewildering detail the vendetta the WSU criminal justice department had launched against him, Michael relaxed. Rather than probe too deeply, he listened with a doting, if somewhat perplexed, complacency. He was convinced that Bryan just needed to vent. This was school stuff—every job has its fair share of politics, right? he would tell himself, friends noted—and he felt assured his smart son would be able to work things out.

THE FIRST TIME BRYAN WALKED through a murder scene was in the old stone house on the leafy corner of Taylor Drive, in Center Valley, Pennsylvania. Bloodstained bodies were sprawled about the musty, low-ceilinged living room. Only the corpses were mannequins, the blood was red paint, the living room was in the DeSales University "crime scene house," and he was an undergraduate taking 365 Psychological Sleuthing.

Bryan was hooked. That was when he made up his mind to switch his focus from psychology and head on to graduate school to study criminology.

As a former addict, he had lived with the awareness that he was one bust away from winding up a criminal; he had, after all, been picked up for making off with his sister's iPhone. And he had known too many from his druggy high school crowd whose lives had become wrapped up in the justice system. But he had turned things around, and now he saw a way of making his reinvention complete. It was a dangerous world, but he'd be a secret hero in the making, one of the good guys who studied crime and criminals. And by digging deep into the criminal world, by studying the theories explaining illegal and deviant behavior, he'd be working with academics who were devising ways to keep crime in check. He'd be an owl, one of the deep thinkers who was determined to make the world a safe place. His mind set, he enrolled for DeSales's online master's degree program in criminal justice.

And that was where he discovered Dr. Katherine Ramsland.

"Serial killers fascinate us. We want to know what makes them tick . . ." she had written. *Inside the Minds of Serial Killers: Why They Kill* was the book, and she seemed to have the answers.

Professor Ramsland, after all, was someone who had done it all. She had a PhD in philosophy (her thesis was on Kierkegaard), had written a small library of books (sixty-eight at last count), had appeared on more than two hundred crime documentaries and television shows, and, most impressively to Bryan, she had actually gotten up close and very personal with a few of the most deviant minds on the planet. When she said serial killers saw the world differently, she was not spouting off like another academic who'd extrapolated her understanding from some dusty texts, but rather as an investigator who had dived straight down into the belly of the beast. When, for example, she wrote about the strange doings inside the mind of Dennis Rader, a convicted serial killer who had murdered at least ten people and who, in a self-aggrandizing flourish, had branded himself with the initials BTK (for "bind, torture, and kill"), Ramsland had firsthand knowledge. For five years, BTK had been communicating with the professor from prison, by phone and in lengthy letters that he'd written in a dauntingly complex code.

But with brains and perspicacity, Ramsland had cracked the code, a psychopath's language where, for unnerving example, "Virals" were victims and "Wheels of Time" referred to what he called "Spin the Bottle," a mind game where women were tied to a torture wheel with their legs spread. She had "gone into the cookie jar," as Rader called his sadistic fantasy world, and when she had emerged, she came out with the "hope others will dig out things that I missed."

Ramsland was a forensic psychologist, a practitioner who applied psychological research and clinical experience to get inside criminal minds. And this was an invaluable skill. Working at the juncture of the legal system and psychology, the forensic psychologist not only could provide a learned assessment of what was going on in a defendant's head, but they might also be able to apply psychology to solve a crime. And Bryan wanted to forge a career at this intellectual crossroad, too. He hoped, as the professor had urged, "to dig out things" she had "missed."

For his master's thesis at DeSales, Bryan set out to emulate Dr. Ramsland by reaching out directly to prisoners. "I am inviting you to participate," he wrote in a survey that he posted on Reddit hoping it would grab the attention of bored convicts, "in a research project that seeks to understand how emotions and psychological traits influence decision making when committing a crime. In particular, this study seeks to understand the story behind your most recent arrest, with an emphasis on your thoughts and your feelings throughout your experience."

And the questions he posed were just the sort of probings that promised rich grist for a forensic psychologist's mill:

Why did you choose that victim or target over others?

Did you prepare for the crime before leaving home?

How did you approach the victim or target?

After arriving, what steps did you take prior to locating the victim or target?

After committing the crime, what were you thinking and feeling?

How did you leave the scene?

How was your life right before the crime?

Michelle Bolger, the associate professor who was Bryan's thesis advisor, was very impressed. Bryan was zeroing in on precisely the sort of questions a forensic psychologist would want to explore. "He was one of my best students, ever. Brilliant," she judged. And so when Bryan asked her for a letter of recommendation for the doctoral program at WSU, she was happy to comply. "In my ten years of teaching," she'd remark, "I've only recommended two students to a PhD program, and he was one of them."

Yet, the time would come when Professor Bolger's thoughts about Bryan would grow troubled, and she would have difficulty sleeping. And now when she reviewed his probing thesis questions in her mind, there was suddenly the possibility that everything she had called brilliance held a more awful promise.

"Fantasy," Dr. Ramsland had written, "also builds to an appetite to experience the real thing."

SIX

———

Bryan, the doctoral student, was the model of ambition. Even before starting classes in the Department of Criminal Justice and Criminology at WSU on August 22, he had already written to the Pullman, Washington, police department applying for an internship.

Doing his best to sound like an academic in the making, Bryan sent an email stating that he "had an interest in assisting rural law enforcement agencies with how to better collect and analyze technological data in public safety operations." Which, when translated, meant he had expertise in gathering evidence from surveillance-camera videos, checking out the cell phones that had pinged off nearby towers as the crime had gone down, and running relevant license plate numbers through the all-knowing law-enforcement computer systems.

The application didn't go anywhere. Perhaps the Pullman PD figured even rural cops had a thing or two on a student when it came to putting the technological pieces together in a crime-solving puzzle. Or maybe they were put off by the applicant's know-it-all tone. But for whatever reason, Bryan didn't get the internship.

Which left him time to concentrate on school. There were thirteen new students in the doctoral program, and he sought them all out. It was a charm offensive, putting on his newly acquired hail-fellow persona as he diligently made the rounds and introduced himself. And he clearly enjoyed being this carefully re-created Bryan. He had never felt so free, so confident. He had flung off the indignities of his past life.

"He definitely seemed a little more eager than some of the others to go around and introduce himself," Ben Roberts, a fellow criminal justice grad student, would recall with what seemed like admiration.

And, as Roberts tells it, Bryan would just chatter away nonstop. Sports, music, his rural Pennsylvania roots—Bryan, out to win friends, was a master of small talk.

While in the classroom, he was a star. He'd plunk himself down front and center, never hiding in the back rows with the trepidatious. He was the student who was always well prepared, who always had his hand raised high, who always had the answer on the tip of his tongue. And when the discussions began, he'd throw himself with gusto right into the mix. Bryan always had something to say, and when spoke, his fellow students listened with attention. "An incredibly strong student," Roberts acknowledged.

His area of specialization—the criminal mind. In class after class, he made it clear that he wanted to follow in the accomplished footsteps of Dr. Katherine Ramsland. Like his mentor, he would specialize in forensic psychology. It was a discipline, he believed, that could open formidable doors concealing dangerous secrets.

Nevertheless, there was one element to the exhilarating show that Bryan was putting on in the seminar classrooms that left many of the students with some disturbing misgivings. And it had little to do with what he said. Nor did it really matter how he said it. Rather, it was his targets.

When any of the female students spoke up, Bryan would go on the attack. He'd rip away at her arguments with a particularly dogged vehemence. A barrage of pointed questions would burst forth. A caustic determination would challenge every assertion. At first it had simply seemed like rudeness, the brightest kid in the class not wanting to share the spotlight with anyone else. But as the term continued and it became clearer that his combative outbursts were only launched against the women in the seminar, people began to wonder if Bryan's taunting was a misogynist's weapon.

THE GOLDEN RULE OF TEACHING is that teachers should treat their students as they would like to be treated. But Bryan, who in return for his fellowship tuition had to put in time as the teaching assistant for Professor John Snyder's undergraduate criminal law sections, had no time for such a commonsense kindness. Why such disregard? Perhaps he had dreamed about having power for so long that, now when it was an actuality, he was determined to savor it. To hear his bullied students tell it, Bryan's arrogance lay deep. His responses to questions about the text or Professor Snyder's lectures were condescending, if not outright mocking, and he enjoyed burying opposing views in a cascade of disdain.

And he didn't stop there. When he corrected student papers, his comments scrawled in the margins were insulting, and the grades were scaled to reflect a perfectionist's demands. "A higher standard," Bryan defiantly called it. It was only a matter of time before the students rose up in revolt.

And they had an ally. Professor Snyder had spent thirty years as a lawyer defending criminal underdogs from charges ranging from simple possession to first-degree murder before joining the WSU faculty. He now convened a session where, under his tacit protection, the students vented their feelings about the low grades they had received. Yet Bryan, still unbowed, still not recognizing the furor that was brewing, gave as good as, if not better than, he got. He was unapologetic. Professor Snyder, by many accounts, kept his thoughts to himself.

But behind the scenes the professor was making it clear that his patience was being tried. Earlier in the term, after the first reports of Bryan's high-hatted antics in the classroom had reached him, Snyder had tried to talk some reason into the young man. The professor was a reasonable, avuncular sort, and he was left astonished when the conversation quickly turned into an argument. And so with a lawyer's orderliness, Snyder started to lay a paper trail that could, if necessary, be produced as the road markers to the brewing disaster. He wrote with concern to Professor Melanie-Angela Neuilly, the department head, whose research field was violence and violent death, to inform her that they might have a loose cannon as a TA. Dutifully, she met with Bryan on October 3 to lay down the law.

But Professor Snyder was not done. On October 21, about midway through the term, he sent Bryan an exhaustive email enumerating "the ways in which you [have] failed to meet your expectations as a TA thus far in the semester."

No doubt Snyder assumed that would shake Bryan up. It might even persuade him to behave more respectfully to his young students and the professor for whom he was working. After all, a lot was at stake. Bryan wouldn't need to read too closely between the lines to gauge the implicit threat: lose your TA job, you also lose your scholarship funding. And without the $26,000 or so needed to cover the annual cost of grad school, Bryan's matriculation at the university would come to an abrupt end.

Bryan was summoned to a powwow on November 2 with Professor Neuilly and Graduate Director Dale Willits. They started out tough, waving the stick: *You'd better shape up or else you're out of here.* After that got the TA's attention, they offered the carrot: *We can still work this out.* They outlined an improvement plan and promised that if Bryan adhered to it, all would be forgiven. His academic life could continue. A chagrined Bryan grabbed the deal.

A month into this truce, as the semester was winding down, a meeting was held to determine if Bryan was fulfilling his side of the bargain. On December 7, Neuilly, Willits, and Snyder sat in a united force on one side of the long table in Johnson Hall; Bryan took his place opposite them. They made Bryan sweat, but the verdict was: "While not perfect," the professors agreed with a muted enthusiasm, "there was progress."

And with that, it seemed Bryan just had to make it through another five days, and then he'd be heading back with his dad to Pennsylvania. His scholarship check for the next semester would be in the mail, and he could return to his TA job in January.

But Bryan apparently would not rest until he had the last word. For just two days later, a self-destructive Bryan, responding to an offhanded criticism from Snyder, unleashed the full force of his considerable fury. In an instant, all the progress the TA had made toward a more professional and respectful demeanor turned to sand. And Snyder was fit to be tied. He reached out once again to the department chair, and she sent an email to Bryan requesting that they meet.

This was, most likely, a summons to the gallows. But before this execution could take place, Bryan quite effectively placed the noose around his own neck: Several of his female students reported to the department that Bryan was making them feel "uncomfortable." In fact, the creepy TA had even followed one of the women to her car.

Now there was nothing further to discuss. Bryan's TA job was over.

Mr. Kohberger. I am writing this letter to formally inform you of the termination of your teaching assistantship with the Department of Criminal Justice and Criminology effective December 31, 2022.

Yet he never received the notice. By the time the letter was mailed to his apartment in Pullman, Bryan had already left campus and was driving back to Pennsylvania with his father.

AND SO ON THE MORNING of December 15, as the Hyundai continued on its way to the enticing Thai restaurant outside Indianapolis, Bryan was avidly explaining to his father that there was no legal way the department would ever be able to strip him of his TA job. Michael had his head craned toward his son, and he was trying, he'd later volunteer, to follow Bryan's diatribe as best he could.

There were rules for an appeals process, Bryan explained. It would be impossible for the department to dismiss him without giving him the chance to have his say. A hearing was necessary. And when he had his day, he was confident that he'd triumph. He had started making an inventory of all the ways he had been wronged, and, he wanted his father to know, he was determined not to walk off without putting up a fight. The students, he complained, had plotted against him because they were too lazy to do the required coursework.

Bryan's diatribe suddenly came to an abrupt halt. It was 10:42 in the morning, and as they approached the 107-mile marker on the interstate, Bryan saw red and blue lights flashing in his rearview mirror. A sheriff's car was demanding that the Hyundai pull over.

Bryan obeyed. He sat behind the wheel, waiting as the officer got out of his vehicle and slowly approached.

And all at once, every fear Michael had been working to keep out of his thoughts seemed inescapable.

PART II

THE CHILDREN'S STORY

On the last evening of her life, Kaylee Goncalves posted this photo on Instagram. "One lucky girl to be surrounded by these ppl everyday." Within hours, four of them would be dead. *Kaylee Goncalves/Instagram*

SEVEN

Everybody's looking for love, right? After all, love is all you
need. At least that's what they keep telling you. So why should you
be any different? You have needs, too.

So you just sit in your room and scroll through FB, or Insta, or
TikTok—and there they are. All of them looking so pretty.

And here's the best part—they don't have any idea you're staring
at them. Following their every post. Checking out every move they
make. Every tasty smile they flash. It's your reassuring secret.

Because if they don't know, they can't turn you down. There's
no one smirking, telling you to get real, dude. There's no one telling
you to get lost.

So you just keep looking and looking and looking.

Only you know what they're thinking: You can't have it!

Want to bet?

As the uniformed police sergeant now slowly approached the
Kohbergers' car, the officer's body cam documented his unhurried
actions. And as it happened, just days earlier, the video of another police
encounter had gone viral on the Internet. Previously overlooked, that
official body cam footage recorded the response to a noise complaint.

A trio of officers had shown up on September 1, 2022, less than two weeks after Bryan, sporting his new swim trunks, had attended the pool party. Like the bash at The Grove, it was another celebration at the start of the new semester. It, too, had taken place in Moscow.

And unknown to either Michael or his son, before the day would be over, a very tight circle of Idaho cops and FBI agents would be reviewing the police body cam videos of the two seemingly unrelated events. They would be searching to discover if an incriminating line of inquiry could be drawn between the recordings. And if they held a clue to the genesis of all the horror that had followed.

WEDGED AGAINST A LEAFY HILLSIDE, the clapboard house at 1122 King Road rose up on three distinct levels from a platform base like an ancient ziggurat. A line of frat houses stretched along a nearby bluff. Beyond that, just across twisting Nez Perce Drive, were the carefully manicured lawns of the University of Idaho campus. September 1 was a Thursday, and pretty much everyone had classes the next day. Nevertheless, by 8:34 that evening, things were going strong inside.

The term had just begun, but 1122 King Road had already secured its reputation as a party house. Tonight it was once again swarming with students. Tyler Childers's "Feathered Indians" boomed from a pair of waist-high speakers, and the music carried aggressively up the block. Revelers called happily to one another, a giddy, drunken mosaic of bouncy, exuberant voices.

Then the cops arrived; for the second time in the past two weeks, an annoyed neighbor had complained about the noise. A police body camera video captured what happened next, and at the time it was seen as only a small, self-contained drama about the push-and-pull tensions between police and students in a college town:

The night is already very dark, as if starless, but the harsh glow of the house lights illuminates a slice of the driveway, and the Moscow PD officers proceed up this marked path. They are heading with determination toward the noise. Yet their progress is suddenly halted. They spot two young women in jean shorts, giggling, leaving the party.

At that moment, the coeds notice them, too. Without a word to one another, acting on pure instinct, they veer off into the darkness. It's as if they know nothing good will come from a confrontation with three cops.

But there is no escape. An officer trains his flashlight on the pair: they are trapped in a cone of yellow light.

"You guys haven't been drinking or anything, right?" he wonders. The mischief in his voice runs high.

"No," the girls reply in a wary, uneasy chorus.

Their interrogator now takes his time. Perhaps he is deciding whether to challenge the response; he could, after all, order a breathalyzer test.

Finally: "Okay, drive careful, okay?" he instructs with a casual authority.

"Thanks," one of the girls offers, while her friend has the wisdom to keep her silence. Relieved, they swiftly rushed off.

"As soon as they know it's the cops . . . they just blend into the darkness." The officer chuckles to his partner. Then they continue up the soft incline toward the house.

"WE'RE ONLY HERE FOR A noise complaint," one of the officers growls, the camera framing his head pitched toward an upstairs window. "Come to the damn door!" he barks. As this new act had opened, he'd been pounding on the white front door for a while, but without any results. His efforts had been rewarded with an aggressive silence.

The cops look up plaintively toward the bright lights of the second-story window. In response, silhouettes dash out of view, apparently finding refuge in the unexposed recesses of the house.

"We'll figure out who lives here eventually," the officer vows to no one in particular.

One of the cops radios the dispatcher. He begins a request for assistance in tracking down the names of the occupants.

This is interrupted, however, when two young men abruptly open the door. The crackle of the walkie-talkie apparently has convinced the students that the cops are determined; they are not going away. The only hope is to defuse the situation before it escalates into something unfortunate.

Both boys are tall, built lean yet broad-shouldered like competitive swimmers, and they deliberately fill the doorway so that the cops cannot look inside. One of them has a white zip tie around his wrist, and the strands of another tie, just remnants, hang loosely from it. It is, no doubt, a proud consolation prize from a recent cuff 'n' chug session. This is a zero-sum fraternity drinking game: two partners are zip-tied together, and whoever first chugs a fifth of liquor can celebrate by cutting himself free (if, of course, his ability to accomplish this task has not become too impaired by the exertions his victory required).

A cop demands to speak to the house's legal tenant, and so the youth with the zip tie obediently disappears inside. But not before firmly closing the door behind him.

How long is he inside? A minute? Maybe less? But to judge by the look of mounting annoyance on the officer's face it might as well have been an hour.

"So I just looked for everyone that lives here, and they're not here right now," the boy announces when he returns at last. His tone is flat, as if he has gone to the trouble of performing a dreary task and now he just wants to be left alone. And the cop cannot help but notice that the student has once again closed the door firmly behind him.

The officer makes a last-ditch effort to restore his control. If the occupants are not present, then perhaps the revelers are all trespassing, he suggests.

Neither of the students appears intimidated. They maintain a detached, untroubled silence.

"Who does live here? What are their names?" the officers ask again, but this time with more force.

Now the second boy speaks up. "I'm not actually sure," he offers unconvincingly. And his friend nods his head, equally baffled.

THE COPS HAVE LITTLE DOUBT they have been lied to by a couple of smart-ass kids. But what can they do? This is Moscow, and the department's policy toward the university is shaped by a shrugging live-and-let-live complacency. As long as no one faces any danger of bodily harm, as long as no major laws are being broken, the edict is to speak loudly, but never let the big stick come crashing down. But that doesn't mean the contempt doesn't grate. The cops discover a backpack stocked with six-packs and Trulys, and they pour the alcohol into the weeds as the video fades out.

BUT NOW, ON THE VERY day when the tall sergeant approached the Kohbergers' car, this months-old grainy video made on a September night in Moscow held the attention of a select group of law-enforcement officials like a magnet. They searched for something they might have previously overlooked. The police scrutinized the heavy shadows that spread around the golden glow of the house on King Road. They were searching for the hiding place of a murderer. The monster who weeks later would kill four young students inside that house.

And so they stopped and started the video dozens of times, poring over the smudges of light and dark in the background. From time to time, they grew encouraged, only to decide with sighs of defeat that their eyes had been playing tricks on them. In the end, anything of evidentiary value—a crouching figure, a peering face, a strategically parked car—eluded them, just as the identities of the occupants of 1122 King Road, despite all the increasingly assertive inquiries, had escaped the officers' knowledge on that night in September.

EIGHT

So who lived at 1122 King Road?

Toward the end of the spring of 2022, as students at the University of Idaho focused on the immediate drudgery of finals while also planning for the future fall term, an enticing advertisement appeared on the websites that hawked local rental housing:

> Fabulous location right next to campus! This 6 Bedroom, 2 Bath three story house has more living space than you'll know what to do with. Tiled entry, large newly updated living room with laminate floors and a great view. Big windows throughout the house and bright, open rooms. Bedrooms offer plenty of privacy with a varied floor plan. Master bedroom has a balcony/deck. Large kitchen has a dishwasher and a sliding door onto a back patio. Washer/dryer available. Large driveway with plenty of off street parking.

The rent for 1122 King Road was $2,095 a month. This was steep for the neighborhood, and particularly daunting to students trying to make ends meet on a makeshift budget. But with all those bedrooms, the monthly nut could be divvied up into a more manageable six slices, and the ten-minute stroll to campus—not to mention the equally pleasing proximity to the social whirl of the nearby frats and sororities—was enticing.

On a warm day early in June, just before they hightailed it out of Moscow for the summer break, six young women appeared at Story Real Estate on Main Street in Moscow to sign the one-year rental agreement for 1122 King Road.

They entered as a group, and they were, it was recalled, particularly quiet, almost solemn. It was as if they were acknowledging the significance of the occasion. The signing of the lease was an important step into adulthood, a tangible symbol of their burgeoning maturity.

The realtor handed them a pen, but they deliberately took their time before taking the final step. One of the girls squeezed another's hand, as if looking for reassurance.

Then, one after another, they signed their names: Ashlin Couch, Bethany Funke, Dylan Mortensen, Madison Mogen, Xana Kernodle, Kaylee Goncalves.

As soon as they were done, Maddie (as her friends called her) let out a small cheer and at once they all started laughing and giggling. All their previous somberness had suddenly vanished and was replaced by elation.

"They were excited," remembered a veteran female realtor who had witnessed the transaction. "The world was their oyster."

TO ANY OUTWARD EYE, THE two ground-floor bedrooms of the house were the least appealing. They were part of the addition that had been tacked on to form the squat base of the house back in 2000, and, apparently, not much thought had been given to the design. Place a bed with a king-sized mattress in the room, and you'd almost need to squeeze sideways to get to the door. And since the windows were smack up against the front driveway, at night the bright headlights of arriving cars would, despite the curtains cloaking the windows, flood the rooms with a blazing illumination.

It's little wonder, then, that one of the young women who had signed the lease and wound up with a ground-floor room quickly decided not to stay. The previous year Ashlin Couch had shared a room at the down-at-the-heels fieldstone-and-clapboard Pi Beta Phi sorority house with another Pi Phi who had convinced her to come along and make the move to King Road for their senior year. At the time, it had seemed like an opportunity worth grabbing.

After all, the Pi Phis were facing a year when any sister wanting serious fun would be well advised to look elsewhere. The chapter had been put on probation by the university's Panhellenic Association for "health and safety reasons." Which was Greek speak, a careful reading of the fine print revealed, for "violations or concerns regarding risk management, alcohol/drugs, or hazing." Going forward, the goings-on in the house would undoubtedly be carefully monitored. And who needed that?

The prospect of a rousing senior year, of turning a glorious twenty-one, far from the prying and censorious eyes of any lurking house mothers, was indeed tempting. And, the icing on the cake, Ashlin's old Pi Phi roommate would be in the new house, too. This was the girl with whom she wore a matching bracelet, self-tanned every Wednesday with a nearly religious allegiance, shared the ritual of making coffee each morning, and, when she needed to let off steam or simply to smile, blasted Usher rapping "Yeah" and danced until they fell down laughing.

Ashlin had signed the lease with great enthusiasm, but after just a couple of nights, she moved out. There was, she told friends, a boyfriend involved. Her mother, who was a canny realtor up north and knew a thing or two about property values, approved the decision, too. A better deal could be had elsewhere, she had counseled. And in time, Ashlin's brief stay—she'd return, though, for one happy night to celebrate her twenty-first birthday with her gang of friends in this party house—became little more than a small addendum to the large tragedy that would forever be attached to 1122 King Road.

STILL, ONE OF THE ORIGINAL leaseholders remained willing to put up with the misery of a basement room. A sophomore, and at nineteen the youngest of the housemates, Bethany Funke might very well have figured that she would get the short end of the stick. She, too, was a Pi Phi, and if the two older Pi Phis in the house had staked their claims to the more appealing rooms, then she had no choice but to go with the flow. Just a year ago she had been a wide-eyed Little, as new sorority members were called, and still felt she owed a measure of sisterly deference to the girls who had preceded her into the hallowed ranks of Pi Beta Phi.

Bethany was a sparky young woman, blessed with the blond good looks that were a God-given ticket for admission to sorority life at the university, and she also had a quick mind. If the price she had to pay for the promise of new off-campus adventures was getting stuck with a poky downstairs bedroom, Bethany didn't complain. In fact, after being shown her gloomy little corner of the house, her initial reaction had been to shrug and say, "How much time will I spend down here anyway?" She had signed on, determined to follow the fun; wherever it was taking shape, that would be her real home.

UP THE NARROW STAIRCASE FROM her room was the merry soul of the house. This was where the parties would inevitably pick up steam, where connections would be made and late-night secrets shared. There was a living room with a slush gray sectional that reeked of stale beer, and conveniently adjacent to it stood a flimsy plastic table with a field of red plastic party cups arranged in a V for the inevitable games of beer pong. High on a far wall hung a cursive neon-lettered sign that might as well have been both a blessing and a precept for all who entered: GOOD VIBES.

Across the hallway was the kitchen, and its sink and Formica countertops were a monument to sloth: a scattering of dirty coffee cups, stacks of cereal bowls that leaned so perilously they seemed destined to topple at any moment, a sticky colander that might very well have been employed weeks ago to drain some spur-of-the-moment pasta, and a jungle of paper bags that had held DoorDash deliveries. And jutting out from the far side of the kitchen was a small, rectangular concrete porch that narrowed to snake around the rear of the house. When one of the speakers was placed out here, the surrounding hills would come alive with the sound of pulsating music.

Conveniently, the porch's sliding glass door provided another entry into the house; you could come in from the grassy slope of woods, a canopy of late-night stars pointing the way, and pop into the kitchen. If it ever occurred to anyone that it might make good sense to go to the trouble of locking this door, they never shared the concern.

Then from the kitchen, it was only a short stroll down one more shoulder-wide hallway to still another corner bedroom. It shared a thin wall with the living room.

THIS WAS DYLAN MORTENSEN'S ROOM. She had been raised by her mom and stepfather in Boise, but it was Brent, her dad, who apparently held center stage in her mind. The twenty-year-old college junior, in fact, had a habit of reposting her father's thoughts on social media. She wanted all her friends to get a measure of the dad she felt lucky to have. And so, for example, she reposted:

"Just a friendly reminder of who is going to show up at the boys [sic] door who messes with one of my daughters."

Fixed below was a photo of a man with dark, glowering eyes and who looked as formidable as the stone façade of the Boise courthouse.

But Brent Mortensen had a softer dad side, too:

"If you ever need anything you let me know. A ride home, clothes, me to be at an event, get you out of trouble, food or just a hug . . . I will drop whatever I'm doing to help you."

Arguably, the two posts were, in their unintentional yet nevertheless revelatory way, a mirror into Dylan, too. Like her dad, she was a tall, striking presence. She had a deliberately unruly mane of blondish hair that would, depending on the season, turn surprisingly light or surprisingly dark. And like all her Pi Phi sisters, she had a classic Barbie oomph: a cheery, straight, even featured face and a shapely body that seemed made for Instagram.

And also like her dad, at least to hear her sorority sisters tell it, she was the sort of young woman you could count on. If you needed a favor—whether you want to borrow a dress or notes from English class—Dylan wouldn't hesitate to accommodate. Friends were always dropping by wanting something, and she'd never disappoint. "A friend in need is a friend indeed," she'd repeat with a benevolent conviction.

At the time, some of her more world-weary Pi Phi sisters simply recoiled with an indulgent sigh at her naïveté. But later, after all that would happen, it would be recalled as something deeply ironic. Or even worse.

NINE

——

And with the neon glow of the GOOD VIBES sign lighting the way, follow the short hallway that shot off in a perpendicular line from the living room and here was the remaining second-floor bedroom. This was Xana Kernodle's tiny dominion.

Xana, unlike the other girls, had needed to follow a much more complicated path to get to college. Her matriculation, in fact, was a miracle of perseverance.

Twenty years earlier, on the day Xana was born, her mother had just received word that she could remove the court-mandated ankle monitor she had been toting around. Cara Kernodle had been picked up on drug charges, but the system had quickly cut her loose and placed her on probation.

Five months later, though, Cara, the new mother, got nabbed again for drugs, and this time the authorities were not so forgiving. She had to serve time. And this would become the dismal recidivist pattern of her life, a morose story documented in the pages of a long rap sheet. There would be more than forty arrests, mostly for possession of drugs or drug paraphernalia. And there were other victims, too: she had been convicted of injury to a child for exposing her two daughters, Xana and her older sister, Jazzmin, to drug use.

Jeff Kernodle, Xana's father, had his fair share of problems, too. He admitted in court that he had used meth and he had also served a short sentence on a drug-related charge. Yet just when it seemed Xana and her sister would become de facto orphans, shuttled off to the misery of a state facility, their aunt Kim rushed in to give the two girls a chance at a better life.

Kim's own children were grown, and her cozy timber home in Post Falls, Idaho, nestled in the towering tree line that climbed up the Coeur d'Alene Mountains, might just as well have come out of a fairytale. Under Kim's steady, benevolent hand, the two young girls got to be two young girls.

And Xana got to indulge a playful, mischievous streak. As a four-year-old, she'd, for example, come upon a can of Crisco in the kitchen and decided to lather the thick white paste all over her body as if it were a lotion, and then paint the bathroom walls with it, too, for good measure. Or she'd deliberately make a racket in her upstairs bedroom knowing that it would be the signal for Auntie Kim to come pounding up the stairs and order her sternly back to bed. Only once she heard the heavy tread of her aunt's feet on the wooden stairs, Xana would rush back under the covers and feign a deep sleep. Kim would play along, pretending to be perplexed by what had caused the noise, while Xana, her eyes closed tight in a make-believe slumber, would struggle to suppress her giggles. It was a lighthearted game they'd play night after night, the aunt and her niece each getting a kick out of milking their respective roles.

Then after a happy two years living under Aunt Kim's protective wing, things got even better for Xana. Her father turned it all around. Jeff got a job in construction, put in backbreaking hours, and soon was able to give the girls a home. And, reunited with their father, they flourished.

Jeff, as if in turn, flourished, too. Now officially divorced from Cara, he started his own firm, Kernodle Construction, and people liked his skilled, often artful work. Clients kept coming with new projects. In time, he was able to move his daughters into a sturdy four-bedroom house with a spacious backyard and a fenced-in front lawn. Shoeshine, their dog, completed this once seemingly unimaginable picture of family happiness.

Xana grew up to be a teenage beauty. She had large, soulful brown eyes, long brunette hair, a soft mocha hue to her skin, and a gymnast's lithe body. Starting in elementary and then all through junior high, she had spent her afternoons after school at the Flip Flop Gymnastics Academy. Most weekends she'd travel to tournaments around the state, the little girl in the blue-and-white leotards, her pigtails of hair tied with bows, and, time after time, a necklace of medals hanging from her neck by the end of the competition.

At Post Falls High, Xana was one of the cool girls, part of the crowd that always had something to do on a Saturday night, that got asked to all the dances. When there was a party, she'd be the one in the half-shirt and shorts, nails painted red, looking not just good but in control. Emily, her bestie, would share a picture of a serious teenager, one carrying herself with a confidence that many found intimidating. *Bring it on!* Xana seemed to be taunting, another friend agreed.

And put Xana on the volleyball court, and you'd see this edge, too. She was always the one jumping high to intercept the ball in midair and then, with a wallop, spike it hard over the net. In high school she lettered in track and soccer, as well as volleyball, and no matter what the sport, Xana played to win. "She hated losing," one of her teammates would remember.

Xana had large ambitions, even if they were still taking shape. One day she'd fantasize with Emily about their dream weddings, the next she'd predict she would always be single. And she wasn't too embarrassed to post on social media, "I would just like to admit that I have no idea what I'm doing." Yet when it was time to get serious, Xana would show her mettle. On the mortarboard she wore to her high school graduation in 2020, amid a decorative drawing of flowers and birds, she pledged with an almost palpable determination, *For the lives I will change.*

When the summer was over, she headed off to the university in Moscow. She had her heart set on being a Pi Phi, and so of course she got in. As for her studies, when it came time to declare a major she'd put down marketing but without any real commitment. She'd repeatedly tell people that you go to college to figure out what you want to do. It was foolishness to have your mind made up at twenty. "Plans fall in the making," she was fond of saying.

In the meantime, she dutifully went to classes, hung out with her sorority sisters, went to party after party along Greek Row, and, to help make ends meet, worked part-time as a waitress at the Mad Greek restaurant, a laid-back student joint on Main Street whose owner had come to Moscow after some years in Alaska.

By the end of her sophomore year, when three of her sorority sisters approached Xana with the idea of moving into the King Road house, she was immediately game. She had reached the stage of her young life when it seemed the time had come to make a clean break from all the annoying rules and overbearing restrictions that came with living in a sorority house. This desire for a life change had been building up for the past year. For to her complete surprise—as well as the delight of her father and sister, who were beginning to fear that it would never happen—Xana had fallen in love.

And Xana, who had been in many ways looking for love since her childhood when both her parents had been taken from her, now loved the only way she knew how: totally.

WHILE XANA'S PARENTS WERE THE sort who, at least in her early childhood, had been separated from their daughters, Ethan Chapin's mother and father had been cut from a different mold entirely. Jim and Stacy Chapin had been set on building a sturdy and affectionate life for their family, and, with a surprising easiness, they had done precisely that, and even a bit more.

The Chapins had an owner's interest in Pacific Belting Supply in

Mount Vernon, Washington. The town was in the northwestern corner of Washington State, plunked down on the snaking banks of the Skagit River and hemmed in by snowcapped mountains and thick evergreen forests. Famously, it was tulip country, carefully planted and tended fields stretching for miles and miles.

The Chapins had a big house in town on a well-kept acre of land. And they also had a getaway home hewn from rough timber logs in northern Idaho just thirty miles from the Canadian border on pristine Priest Lake. This, the locals would swear with deep conviction, was God's country, and by that they meant it was still pretty much as God made it.

Yet best of all, the Chapins had a nearly instant family ready to fill the many rooms of their homes with laughter, horseplay, and, for years, the discordant sounds of novices making their way through the twelve major clarinet scales. The Chapins had three children, and each was born nearly precisely one minute after the other. Ethan came first, followed by his brother, Hunter, and sister, Maizie.

Since Ethan was the oldest of the triplets, even if by only minutes, perhaps it was only natural that he was their leader. They all played sports, lived for sports to hear their mom talk about it, but Ethan was always the star no matter what the game. That was true in soccer, where all three, the two boys and their sister, played on the same Conway Middle School team in Mount Vernon. And at Mount Vernon High School, the two boys played basketball. Both were forwards, but Ethan, who as a sophomore was already a towering six four (his brother an inch shorter), had been a Skagit County all-star year after year.

Yet broad-shouldered, hulking Ethan was, his friends would tease, a "Gentle Giant." He didn't so much stride as shuffle about, never, it seemed, in a hurry. And nothing could upset him; he'd always shrug setbacks off with an easy, affable grin. And so when Covid pretty much shut down his high school for both his junior and senior year and classes were online (not that he ever had too much truck with academics), he adjusted in his usual, compliant way. Instead of going to school, he worked long hours furrowing and seeding in the tulip fields. Or he'd head up to Priest Lake and bus tables at Hill's Resort.

Still, he didn't let Covid put too much of a damper on his socializing. He found time to be the slightly goofy, often tipsy clown, dancing in a women's bikini top, or playing beer pong dressed up as a hot dog. He was always the first on the dance floor, cutting his moves with an exaggerated playfulness. Ethan was the life of every party, and that was just how he wanted it to be.

But by the time Ethan (along with his brother and sister) had arrived at the University of Idaho in August 2021 for his freshman year, the Gentle Giant had grown up into a handsome young man, with a mop of thick dark hair; a wide, thoughtful forehead; sleepy brown eyes; and a sly hipster's mustache. Ethan projected a calm, unflurried assurance, a steady contentment.

In his happy-go-lucky, ready-to-party way, Ethan was a fraternity guy before he had ever signed on. But once at the university, he rushed (along with his brother, Hunter) Sigma Chi. His sister, Maizie, had joined the stately, rather decorous Kappa Alpha Theta sorority. But Sigma Chi, a blue ranch house perched on a bluff along Nez Perce Drive, was Ethan's kind of place—a big, disheveled man cave. The bunk beds were squeezed together in closet-sized rooms nearly side by side, and if you were unfortunate enough to get stuck with the upper level and fail to remember to duck when you pulled yourself out of bed to rush to class, you could do serious damage to your head. The bathrooms, seemingly last cleaned during the Clinton administration, were as inviting, if not as toxic, as a nuclear waste dump. The living room was dark, dingy, and reeked of stale beer. And the insouciant brothers were constantly forgetting to feed their house dog, a husky named Bolt.

But the frat had a reputation for throwing bustling parties on a Saturday night. And Ethan, true to his convivial nature, was always the lighthearted giant holding center stage on the dance floor.

It was at one of these frat house gatherings that, toward the end of their freshman year, Xana and Ethan met. Like many romances, it started first as a friendship. They were two young good-looking kids, and they were cautiously taking their time to know one another. Nevertheless, by their sophomore year, they had become, without much drama, a couple.

On a warm spring day they'd go out golfing with friends on the university course and Ethan would open his bag to reveal he'd left his clubs back at the frat house and had instead stocked up on six-packs of Bud Light Lime, his drink of choice. Or Xana, now pretty much part of the family, would come up to the Chapins' summer home in Priest Lake, and there she'd be at the dinner table talking away with Stacy Chapin as Jim carried in the grilled burgers and hot dogs.

Photo after photo, no matter where they were taken, caught the identical pose: Xana nestled under the protective crook of Ethan's arm, her head resting blissfully on his broad shoulder.

There was one photograph, however, that was Xana's favorite. She kept it in a drawer in her room in the house on King Road. It was a shot of Ethan standing tall in a bright field of tulips at a farm not far from his family's Skagit Valley home. She cherished it because Ethan had told her that tulips, according to Turkish tradition, were considered "a symbol of enduring love."

And she had happily taken that knowledge to heart. But if Xana had done a bit more probing, she would have discovered that the Dutch had a different view. For them, tulips symbolized the briefness of life.

TEN

Which left the third floor of the house. And here at the summit were the two bedrooms that were the shared domain of Kaylee Goncalves and Madison Mogen. Divvying up the top floor that way seemed only natural; the two twenty-one-year-olds had grown up sharing pretty much everything.

It was as if the two girls had been born under the same star—same age; same schooling; same cute short-skirt, tight-faded-jeans fashion sense; same bubbly one-hundred-watt smile; same long, cascading blond hair (although Kaylee's shiny yellow color owed a lot more to nurture than nature). At a quick glance, the only immediately noticeable difference was that Maddie was petite, a pint-sized yet no less glam version of her best friend. To just about everyone who knew them, it was as if they were two parts of one whole. Their names might just as well have been hyphenated: Kaylee-Maddie.

The two girls had met in the sixth grade at the Coeur d'Alene Charter Academy. It was a proudly rigorous school and provided a no-nonsense college-prep education. It offered, the school administrators would brag, a chess club but no football team. Magazines repeatedly ranked it the best secondary school in the state. And it hadn't taken long before Kaylee-Maddie were champing at the bit to get out.

They had arrived at the school by different, outwardly incompatible paths. Kaylee had grown up the giggling, high-spirited middle child in a family of five. Of the brood, she was the daredevil, the one who would lie flat on the ground as the garage door descended like a guillotine and, as her siblings cheered her on, wait until the last possible moment to roll to safety. And she was the prankster, the one who removed the batteries from the TV remote and then watched with suppressed laughter as her grandfather ranted about how the darn thing was inexplicably broken. It was a happy home, and a happy childhood.

Her father, Steve, had studied computer science and played football at the University of the Pacific in California and then gone on to earn a good living bouncing from one IT job after another. With his wife, Kristi, they first owned a rambling house on a suburban tree-lined street right near the shores of Lake Coeur d'Alene. Then, their hearts set on living in the country, the Goncalveses bought a seven-acre spread with pastures and woods and a house large enough for each of the kids to have their own bedroom in nearby Rathdrum. In time, they added a pool to make things even more perfect.

For Maddie, childhood was a more grinding time. Ben and Karen Mogen's marriage had cracked from the strains caused, in part, by Ben's drug use and the all too frequent struggle to pay bills. They separated when Maddie was a toddler. (In the decades to come, Ben would still be pleading guilty to misdemeanor drug raps, and going off to do ninety days in jail; and his new wife, Kori, Maddie's stepmother, would face drug charges, too.)

Karen remarried Scott Laramie, and now Maddie, trying to make the best of things, called both Ben and her new stepfather "Dad." She grew up in a working-class neighborhood in a small, tight house on Lacrosse Avenue in Coeur d'Alene. It was a bit down-at-the-heels, and in fact it looked like it could use a fresh coat of paint, but, same as nearly everywhere in Idaho, there wasn't too long of a hike to a shimmering lake or a grove of evergreen trees. Maddie liked to pretend she was a fairy. It didn't matter if things were rocky at home; she could escape to the twinkling magic of her inner life.

But once she met Kaylee, it was as if there was no longer any need to escape to a splendid imaginary world. Maddie now had the real thing. And it wasn't just her wonderful Bobbsey Twins–like friendship with Kaylee. The Goncalveses had taken her into their family, too. They routinely set another place for her at the dinner table when she came over after school to do homework. And Maddie joined in when it was time to put the ornaments and tinsel on the tall Christmas tree in the living room. When they went off on family vacations—and the Goncalveses made a point of escaping whenever they could from the long, brutal Idaho winters—they took Maddie along. From Belize to Cabo to Waikiki, the two girls posed for family snapshots in their bikinis in one glistening tropical holiday backdrop after another. The Goncalveses would both say that they grew to think of Maddie as another daughter.

And the bonds only grew stronger—between both sets of parents as well as the girls themselves—after Kaylee-Maddie presented their "proposal."

It was a well-thought-out document. The two coconspirators had spent a lot of time huddled in Kaylee's room refining their arguments and zeroing in on the proper firm, but at the same time noncombative, tone. It was midway through their eighth-grade year and their minds were made up: they had had enough of the demanding Charter Academy and wanted out. Instead, they hoped to transfer to Coeur d'Alene's Lake City High, where they wouldn't be required to wear ugly old-lady khaki skirts and on Friday nights they could cheer on the Timberwolves with the rest of the town. And the prospect of a more manageable homework load was pretty enticing, too.

After the parents read the coauthored document, they were too impressed to put up much of a fight. And besides, they wanted their daughters to be happy.

Kaylee-Maddie were indeed happy at Lake City. Without trying very hard, they did well in their studies, and had time for active social lives as well as family vacations. They went to parties and to proms. They cheered on the Timberwolves during Spirit Week and wore short black dresses to the homecoming dance. On graduation day, they posed side by side on the green grass of the football field in their purple gowns, both wearing similar white dresses underneath. Kaylee grasped a pink bouquet in her hands because pink was Maddie's favorite color. *I wouldn't have wanted anyone else to be the main character of my childhood years*, Kaylee wrote under Maddie's yearbook photo. And Maddie replied, *I love you more than life! My best friend forever and more.*

Then in August, together of course, they were off to the University of Idaho.

BUT THEN SOMETHING UNPREDICTABLE HAPPENED: Maddie pledged Pi Beta Phi and, against all expectations, Kaylee joined Alpha Phi. Both were party houses, and both attracted the type of young women who, to an outsider's admiring eye, seemed impressively poised and confident. So why had Kaylee-Maddie finally decided to put a pause in their hyphenated existence? The answer might very well lay in the critical mindsets of the sorority members who were doing the choosing. The girls might not have received offers to join the same sorority. But many people came to believe that the decision was, at its core, of the girls' own doing. They had come to college eager to spread their wings, and the only way to soar, they had decided, was to fly off on their own.

For the first three years at the university, while they remained best friends, they also enjoyed new, independent lives. Their sororities kept them busy. And they were both industrious students. Kaylee was enrolled in the university's College of Letters, Arts and Social Sciences, and she was breezing through it with flying colors. In fact, she'd taken sufficient additional courses each term and done so well that she planned to graduate early, at the end of the fall term of her senior year.

Maddie, who was a marketing major, made the dean's list every semester, and accomplished this feat while working part-time as a wait-ress at the Mad Greek downtown in Moscow and also handling the PR and marketing duties at Pi Beta Phi.

And there was something else that couldn't help but drive them further into their own worlds: they had each fallen in love. And like all true first loves, it made everything else in their lives seem trivial.

ELEVEN

Bid night at a sorority is about new beginnings. It's the evening when the pledges, having passed all of their elders' discerning tests, officially accept the invitation to join the elite. And at the rambling Pi Phi house on the corner of Ash Avenue, it was always an ebullient, even triumphal event. The excited new "Littles" would put on their CITY OF ANGELS T-shirts (back in the 1930s, crooners in raccoon coats had sung adoringly about Pi Beta Phi angels, and nearly a century later the seraphic image was still invoked), and then they would head off on the town with their "Bigs."

And as if confirming the complete rightness of all upon which she was now embarking, on bid night, when Maddie joined her new sisters to toast her now official affiliation with the Pi Phis, she met Jake Schriger. And just like that, another new beginning took hold in her freshman year and shook her young life.

Schriger had also gone to Lake City High in Coeur d'Alene, but he was a couple of grades ahead of Maddie. Their paths had never crossed until now. Jake was good-looking, trim in an athletic sort of way, strong-featured, and fair-haired, and he was a Delta Tau Delta, and like all Delts he had a reputation on campus as a cool guy. By the end of the evening, friends would recall with knowing smiles, Jake was directing his charm straight at Maddie and, just as intently, she was taking it all in.

They were two serious young people—in fact, that was, Maddie would tell people, what attracted her to Jake—and their courtship had, at least in its early days, a calm, measured pace. They hung out together, but usually in the protective company of the group of Pi Phis who would regularly gather at Jake's off-campus apartment. Come summer, Maddie would tag along with him on the four-hour drive down to McCall, Idaho, a picture-postcard resort town on the shores of Payette Lake. Jake owned a power boat and he'd captain it around the lake as Maddie stretched out on the deck taking in the rays. And all the time they would be talking. Maddie would tell people there was nothing they couldn't talk about. But, of course, there was one thing, and they both laboriously pretended not to notice its hovering, yet unarticulated, presence.

"She knew her worth," Jake, with a business major's practicality, would put it. "I had to work for her," he admitted.

Their first official date was Valentine's Day, and they went to the Breakfast Club on Main Street in Moscow. The Club's an easygoing, artsy place where students can nurse a strong latte as they sit hunched over their laptops. It's not the most romantic of venues. But by this point in their long-running friendship, both Maddie and Jake had stretched their defenses threadbare, and so when Jake blurted out that he had fallen in love with her, Maddie happily surrendered. "Me too," she agreed.

And that settled that. They'd cuddle up under a blanket to watch football games or *The Princess Bride*. They went to country music festivals, and Maddie wore her pink cowgirl boots. And they liked to hug. "They were peanut butter and jelly," said Jake's mom.

They both knew it would last forever.

KAYLEE, MEANWHILE, HAD ALSO GOTTEN caught up in something that might very well last forever, only the possibility scared the hell out of her. To a young woman who had no inclination to suppress either her keen taste for adventure or her smoldering ambition, forever stretched ahead like a jail sentence.

She had met Jack DuCoeur in high school, and he had asked her to the senior prom. Kaylee was ecstatic. Jack was the type of popular, big man on campus many girls at Lake City would have been eager to have on their arm. Red-haired and wiry, he was a tennis player, second singles on the Lake City team, and he'd been good enough to earn a place in the North Idaho Athletic Hall of Fame. He also was a juggler, having trained since he was a kid with the Levity Juggling Group in Coeur d'Alene. He could keep a handful of tennis racquets circling simultaneously through the air. Or he and a cohort would play a fast-paced game of catch with a torrent of whizzing clubs. It always seemed quite impossible, but he managed to pull it off.

Jack went off to the university in Moscow same as Kaylee, and, like his girlfriend, he embraced the Greek life. And Kaylee and Jack were a couple. Except when they were not. One day they bought a milk-chocolate-brown goldendoodle, christened him Murphy, and decided he was the cutest thing in the world. The next they'd be fighting over who got custody of the dog. Friends would say they'd each had the misfortune of meeting the right person too soon. As a consequence, a volatile pattern emerged. They'd break up only to soon make up. Then the cycle of resentment and recrimination, followed close on its heels by regret, would start again. Yet for all their defiant talk, neither of them had ever run too far from each other.

And as she prepared to head into her senior year, Kaylee found her inevitable way back to her best friend. She decided to join Maddie and two of her friend's Pi Phi sisters and move into the house on King Road. Not that she planned to be there very long. Her mind was still set on graduating in December; she had sufficient credits. And hand in hand with that decision, Kaylee had also found the will to once and for all end her relationship with Jack.

She had played out this entanglement for five complicated years, and when she searched her soul, she realized that all it had offered was an excuse not to engage in the larger world that was waiting beyond campus, or, for that matter, Idaho. With this new understanding, she forged an audacious plan. After Christmas, she'd head off backpacking through Europe. Then she'd return to a job at a marketing firm in Austin, Texas; she had already been accepted, and would start in February. That, she rejoiced, would be the true start of the next chapter of her life.

And so it was that not long after the fall term had begun, she had for all ostensible purposes moved out of the King Road house and returned to Coeur d'Alene. She had found a well-paying job and was building a nest egg. Everything in her new, purposefully crafted life was, to Kaylee's delight, falling into place.

And now she had a surprise she wanted to share with Maddie.

"You have any plans for the weekend of November 12?" Kaylee asked her best friend. "How about I come down to Moscow?"

"It's a football weekend. A lot will be happening. We'll have a great time!" Maddie gushed. She was immediately thrilled by the prospect of a reunion, her friends would say.

"Awesome," Kaylee agreed. And she teased, "I have something I want to show you."

TWELVE

Even with some years and miles on it, the Range Rover Evoque was a very flashy car. True, the Evoque was, as the brochures put it with heavy tact, the "entry-level" Land Rover model, and there was no pretending a six-year-old vehicle had come straight out of the showroom. But for someone wanting to make a statement in a college town, a Range Rover, age or model be damned, could hardly be improved upon.

And so on the afternoon of November 11 when Kaylee pulled up to the white front door of 1122 King Road at the wheel of her newly leased silver 2016 Evoque, who could blame her if she felt it was the ideal way to make an entrance? She was moving on from her college days, and doing it in style.

This was the surprise she had been so eager to share with Maddie and, by all accounts, the car caused quite a stir. And not just with her best friend, but with the other girls, too. It struck them as astonishing that a roommate (although she spent most of her time up in Coeur d'Alene, Kaylee had kept her third-floor room through graduation in December) had been able to handle the cost of such an extravagance. The down payment? The monthly lease? Those were serious, real-world bills. And staring enviously at the spiffy silver gray car, they might very well have feared a gulf larger than the eighty-five miles between Moscow and Coeur d'Alene had opened up between Kaylee and them.

They needn't have worried. It was just like old times.

MOST WEEKENDS IN MOSCOW DURING the fall term played out with the rhythm of a three-day party, and this was even more so when there was a football game at Kibbie Dome. On Saturday, the Vandals would be playing their first home game of what so far had proven to be a surprisingly successful season. The prospect of a win against UC Davis—and an invitation down the road to the division championship playoffs?—helped fuel the upbeat mood.

For the residents of King Road, it was a time for both dressing up and going out. On Friday night, Kaylee tagged along as Dylan's plus-one to the Pi Phi formal. Kaylee, although an Alpha Phi, would have known just about everyone at the gathering and would have had no trouble comfortably fitting in. She was PPB, as the appreciative Greek Row shorthand put it: pretty, popular, and blond.

And later, the roommates returned home and no doubt talked late into the night as only friends without secrets can.

BY ALL ACCOUNTS, THE NEXT day got off to a late start; it was the weekend, and once the morning coffee had worked its restorative magic, someone had an inspired idea. "Who knows when we'll all be together again?" the instigator, destined to be forever anonymous, challenged. "We should preserve the moment. Take a photo."

In the bright autumnal light, the roommates all lined up on the narrow porch at the back of the house in a shoulder-to-shoulder row.

At each end of the row, as if bookends to the larger drama that was already taking its inevitable shape, were Dylan and Bethany. While at center stage, directly in the camera's eye, were the other four.

Little Maddie was balanced on Kaylee's shoulders, blonde on blonde, united and dependent on each other. Once again a single, hyphenated unit: Kaylee-Maddie. Standing next to them, a head taller, was a tousled-haired Ethan grinning his engaging jack-o'-lantern smile. His left arm was crooked possessively and protectively around Xana, both of their dark outfits outliers to the faded denims all the others were wearing.

Later that evening—at 8:57, to be precise—Kaylee posted the photo on her Instagram account. "One lucky girl to be surrounded by these ppl everyday."

THE FOOTBALL GAME WAS OVER—THE Vandals had lost badly—but now it was evening, and the weekend nevertheless rolled merrily along.

Ethan, the dutiful triplet, was his sister's date at Kappa Alpha Theta's Bettie Dance. This was the annual fall formal celebrated to honor Bettie Locke Hamilton, one of the sorority's founders. Yet because back in 1867 Bettie had established a dry sorority and the harsh prohibition still ruled more than a century later, the festivities ended mercifully early so that the young people could head out to get a drink. Or three. For starters.

Ethan, looking debonair in his dark suit jacket and a white shirt rakishly unbuttoned in a deep V, had left the formal by 8:00 p.m. to pick up Xana. An hour later they were heading up the hill from the house on King Road to Ethan's frat. At Sigma Chi, it wouldn't be a problem that both of them, just twenty, were under the state's legal drinking age. And they hurried because they were late. No matter what the time, people liked to snigger, at Sigma Chi the party had already started the night before.

As for Kaylee and Maddie, they had their own plans for the evening. At just after ten, a cab picked them up at the house, and their destination, all things considered, seemed a strange choice. Moscow offered any number of bars; head downtown, and you could make a pleasant time of it in Mingles, or the Dirty Goat, or John's Alley, to cite just a few. On a football Saturday night, any of them would be packed elbow to elbow with students and hard-drinking locals. But Kaylee-Maddie had their hearts set on going to the Corner Club on the northern outskirts of Main Street.

Arguably, the attraction was the Club itself. It was a rah-rah sports bar, a place where, regardless of the season, a game would always be on one of the TVs. And its tie to Vandals football ran deep: every year the homecoming king and queen would hoist themselves up onto the tin-plated bar and burst into the college's fight song: "Came a tribe from the North, brave and bold / Bearing banners of silver and gold . . ."

It seemed, therefore, an appropriate place to drown sorrows over the disheartening Vandals loss. And there were always the Club's famous "Tub Cups," brimming with a hefty thirty ounces of beer; a few of those might take the sting out of any loss on the field.

Another selling point: the Club was a safe place, a hallmark that would not have been overlooked by two attractive women going out on their own on a Saturday night. The bartenders and the locals took a paternalistic view toward the coeds. Kaylee and Maddie wouldn't have had to worry about getting hit on by obnoxious jocks or entitled frat boys. All they'd have to do—and it had, in fact, been demonstrated to them with impressive efficacy in the past—would be to let any of the staff know that some guy was creeping them out, and a giant's arm would be placed with an unmistakable force around the offender's shoulder as he was ushered out the metal front door and into the street.

Looking at things that way, the Corner Club would have been a logical, even a prudent choice for the two women.

Except it wasn't. There was one additional detail that, in any rational world, should have made the bar decidedly off-limits.

All weekend, Kaylee had been insisting it was permanently over between Jack DuCoeur and her. And if anyone had the temerity to suggest otherwise, Kaylee would shoot back with an unwavering certitude. "This is it!" she had repeatedly vowed.

Yet if that was truly the unalterable state of their union, then Kaylee would have been wise not to go into the Club even if it were the only bar in town. For on a Saturday night, the bartender was certain to be Adam Lauda. He was a hunky, six-foot-five basketball player, and a Delt. But most significantly, he was Jack DuCoeur's roommate, frat brother, and best buddy. With Adam behind the bar, it was a sure thing that Jack would be there drinking, too.

Which meant her heading out to the Corner Club made no sense. Unless, of course, as it was later suggested by those who knew her well, a considerable motivating factor in her decision to return to Moscow for the weekend had been to reconnect with Jack. Even if Kaylee wouldn't admit it to herself.

Still, once the two girls joined the swirl of drinkers crowded into the Club, Kaylee did her best to stick to her guns. The bar was jammed, and so it was easy to keep her distance from Jack. They shared a few words, and in the judgment of those who had witnessed the exchanges, they seemed little more than polite, if not downright terse.

Maddie, though, had apparently seen through all her best friend's self-deceptions. She spent a large part of the evening huddled at the bar with Lauda, no doubt probing his assessment of where things truly stood between Kaylee and Jack. And who could blame her if she was set on seeing her friend happy?

Then it was past 1:00 a.m., closer to 1:30 by some accounts, and, a little worse for drink but happily so, the two young women left the bar.

THE NOVEMBER NIGHT WAS CLEAR and frosty and full of stars. Yet they walked down Main Street as though oblivious to the cold. Kaylee's jeans were fashionably ripped at the knees, and she wore only a sweatshirt for warmth. Maddie, in frayed jeans and a pink top that stopped well above her navel and left a generous amount of flesh exposed, had on a black zippered jacket, several sizes too big—the sleeves nearly reached her knees. She wore it unzipped, playfully flopping the absurd long sleeves about as if she were a bird testing her wings before taking to flight.

Following behind them at a decorous distance was Jack Showalter. He was someone they knew from around campus, and when they left the bar he had tagged along. Perhaps they thought it was a protective gesture, an acquaintance keeping a watchful eye as they sauntered down Main Street in the sharp, dark night. Or maybe they found his trailing them an annoyance.

Regardless, the two women paid him no mind. Kaylee's thoughts were elsewhere. "Maddie! What did you say to Adam?" she demanded.

It was as if she feared her friend had been probing the bartender about Jack DuCoeur.

"Like, I told Adam everything . . ." Maddie conceded.

That seemed a sufficient explanation. At once Kaylee stopped delving into such raw territory. And besides, she had her pride, and Showalter was lurking.

By now they had made their way to the Grub Truck. Parked kitty-corner to Main Street, the truck provided the tipsy college kids with the opportunity to soak up a bit of the evening's alcohol with a variety of leaden mac-and-cheese dishes or a berry Nutella cheesecake burrito.

"Carr-ban-ara," Kaylee ordered as if she were mouthing a tongue twister; alcohol could make the simplest of things a struggle.

They puffed clouds of frosted breath into each other's faces as they waited for the food they'd share. Maddie looked very small inside the big black coat.

Abruptly, she turned toward Showalter. His hood was now pulled over the ball cap on his head and he stood in the shadows talking quietly to another guy. "Fuck you!" Maddie declared.

She might have been talking to Showalter. Or she might have been sharing her inebriated resentment about nothing in particular.

At last the food came, and Kaylee, knowing it would be a foolishness to walk the mile or so back to King Road in the bitter cold, had called the number the sororities had previously distributed to hire late-night rides. Without a word to any of the crowd of kids hovering by the food truck, they got into the car and went home.

———

IT WAS 2:00 A.M., AND the house was full. Everyone had come home. Dylan and Bethany had been the first to return; they had gotten back around midnight and now were in their rooms, the doors closed. Xana and Ethan had arrived at about 1:45 a.m. Their footsteps in tandem, they had trudged down the hill from Sigma Chi, walked through the crumpled cans of Keystone beer scattered across the driveway, and settled into Xana's room on the second floor. Kaylee had decided to crash in Maddie's room; Murphy was curled up in the bedroom across the hall.

Unable to sleep, Kaylee's mind refused to rest. Or was it her heart? Had she realized at the end of a long day that all her scrupulously correct behavior at the Corner Club was worth nothing—no, less than nothing? She called Jack at 2:26 a.m. He didn't answer, and within thirty minutes, she had called another six times. All the calls went straight to voicemail. Then, full of a newfound urgency, had she recruited Maddie to reach out to Jack to help make things right? All that is definitively known is that Maddie, once Kaylee had given up, had also tried to phone Jack. Three times in rapid succession. But she, too, had no success; her attempts went unanswered. And so by 3:00 a.m., assuredly frustrated, they were, at last, ready to call it a day.

Xana, though, was not ready for bed. Earlier, at around midnight, she had called her dad to let him know that she and Ethan would be leaving the party soon and heading home. But once back in her room with Ethan, she was still revved up. She scrolled through TikTok. Then she decided she was hungry. She placed a DoorDash order for a cheeseburger and fries from Burger King. The driver had to make the trip to King Road from across the state line in Pullman, ten miles or so away. But at 4:00 a.m. he knocked on the front door and handed Xana a brown paper bag containing her order. She carried it upstairs.

And then the night came falling down with a madness all of its own.

THIRTEEN

———

It is 3:30 in the cold, starlit Sunday morning, November 13, and the quiet on King Road is all enveloping. A whisper, it seems, would echo like a scream.

A white car appears, and it is in no hurry. It creeps along in front of 1122 as though on tiptoes. Continuing past the adjacent Queen Apartments, it climbs up the incline and is abruptly trapped in a dead end. But there's no sense of any frustration. The driver carefully executes a three-point turn, and the car exits toward Greek Row.

Is that it?

The driver cannot seem to find the will to park. He needs to stop wavering and hold the idea, the possibility, firmly in his mind. Only the driver of the white car is unreconciled. He is not there yet. But he *so* wants to because, as if summoned, he returns. The white car retraces its earlier route. But apparently he still cannot vault to the place he wants, he feels he must, reach. He can still see other possibilities. Once again, the white car exits the neighborhood.

Yet minutes later, the car returns as if pulled by an invisible force.

He needs to find the boldness to act. Except he cannot. Once again the car approaches, only finally to pull away.

And this time he is determined to stay away. It's as if he does not want to be that other person. He continues onto Taylor Avenue until King Road is a faint, distant blur in his rearview mirror. He is escaping. But he cannot help himself. It is 4:00 in the morning, and the driver turns around and returns a third time.

The white car has stopped, engine idling, on the asphalt parking bluff above the King Road house. Turning off the ignition will require the strength of Hercules. It seems an impossible task. It's still not too late to flee.

But he must know his hesitation is a hoax. He must understand that only the deed will silence the voices screaming like a chorus of banshees inside his head.

With that realization, self-restraint crumbles. And in an incredible moment, he finds the will. The idea has become as natural as breathing. He is committed. He turns the ignition off. The door of the white car opens. No one notices. All remains still.

A dark figure walks down the dirt incline, the ground hard with a thin coating of frost. He is heading toward the back of the house. In his gloved hand he is gripping a leather sheath that holds a Ka-Bar knife with a sharp, seven-inch steel blade. It is a killer's weapon.

THE SLIDING GLASS DOOR TO the kitchen is rarely locked, and tonight is no exception. The door glides open easily, making only a muffled sound, as slight as a sudden intake of breath, and he steps inside.

Does he listen for a telltale noise? Does he need a moment to get accustomed to this new manner of darkness? Or is the faint glow of the neon GOOD VIBES sufficient to light the way?

Once in the kitchen, he proceeds up the narrow staircase to the third floor. And this is, arguably, telling. If he were aimless, driven only by furious emotions, he would burst forward into either of the second-floor bedrooms. But he has a plan. He knows where he is going. He is a hunter stalking his prey.

Another speculation: since Kaylee no longer lives full-time in the house, his target has always been, since the madness first crept into his thoughts, petite Maddie.

The stairs up to the third floor creak with the tread of his feet. He advances toward the bedroom door. Does his heartbeat slow? Does he feel invulnerable? Does he restrain himself, knowing that attack blows are better for this moment of delay?

When he opens the door, he finds two girls in the bed asleep. He slashes away swiftly, savagely. The wounds are long and very deep. It is quick, vicious work. In the single bed, the two lie dying, their bodies splayed yet touching. Their blood seeps into the mattress in a spreading red stain. Yet despite her wounds, Kaylee manages to lift herself up and, as if trying to escape, wedges herself into the far corner of the small room. The determined killer closes in, and she fights back. But all is quickly over, and her bloody body crumples to the floor.

The commotion and smell of blood rouses the dog, Murphy. From the room across the hall, the dog is frantic, his sense of danger keen. He bellows with large, cathartic howls.

Downstairs, Dylan wakes. Is Kaylee playing with Murphy at this time of night? She calls out with disapproval into the darkness from her bed.

No one answers, but Murphy has calmed in some measure. The sounds the dog makes are steady and low.

The killer walks down the stairwell.

Xana is awake. "There's someone here!" she cries out, the alarm loud enough so that from her bedroom across the hall Dylan hears every word. She opens her bedroom door and peers out. There is only darkness, and, closing the door behind her, she returns to her bed. This is not the time, she decides, to make sense of things.

But Ethan has emerged from Xana's room to investigate. And suddenly he is standing face-to-face with an intruder dressed entirely in black, a black mask pulled up high on the ridge of his nose. Ethan is six four, powerful, an athlete. Yet the killer does not hesitate. He lashes out without compunction, and an arcing blow slices through Ethan's neck, catching the jugular. His body starts to topple, and then falls in the doorway with a flat thud. Does the killer crouch over his victim and continue his attack? If so, the assault is unnecessary. Ethan is already dead.

Xana is sobbing.

The plaintive sound rouses Dylan again. She opens her bedroom door a crack and once again peers. The darkness reveals nothing.

The killer is now close enough to Xana to see that she is trembling. Despite everything that is raging in him, he selects his words with a deliberate care. "It's okay, I'm going to help you," he says.

It is a lie. He has only come to help himself.

He raises his knife and attacks.

From behind her partially opened door, Dylan hears the killer speak. Nothing is making sense. She closes the door and retreats back to her bed.

Xana, 5'3" and 113 pounds, is fighting for her life. But she is no match for the killer. He plunges his knife in deep, again and again. She crumples to the floor. Then he steps over Ethan's body and walks out of the room.

His gait is unhurried. There were four of them, and he never hesitated. He did what he had to, and he must feel exhilarated. He continues back toward the slider door in the kitchen. His self-absorption is total. He never notices that Dylan is standing in the doorway, the bedroom door flung open. And she is staring directly at him as if in a trance.

She sees a man dressed all in black, a black mask reaching up high on his face. As she processes the moment, she decides he is about five ten, maybe taller. Not muscular, but well put together like an athlete. For some reason, her eyes fix on his bushy eyebrows.

She stares at him. A visitor? An intruder? She doesn't understand what has happened. And she is extremely tired. She closes the door of her room and goes to bed, the blanket pulled up high.

Did the killer see Dylan? Does he spare her in a sudden act of kindness? Or at that wild moment is he incapable of seeing anything? It remains a mystery.

He retraces his steps, making his way back up the hill. He is transformed. He has become what he had to become. In little more than eight minutes, ten at most, he killed four people. He gets back in the white car and drives off as the faint light of the new day begins to filter through the lead-gray sky, and the blood spreads in thin red rivulets through the house on King Road.

FOURTEEN

————

As it happened, it was also a white automobile that a sheriff's patrol car, nearly one month to the day after the four murders on King Road, had pulled over to the right shoulder along a stretch of the interstate just past Indianapolis. It was 10:42 in the morning, the sky was bright, and in this sharp light the faces of Bryan Kohberger at the wheel and his father, Michael, in the front passenger seat of the white Hyundai Elantra were clear through the windshield. Bryan sat as still as a statue, his shoulders high, hands hanging at his sides, his eyes fixed on the rearview mirror reflecting the flashing red and blue lights of the patrol car parked directly behind them. Michael had rolled down his window, studying Sergeant Nick Ernstes as he approached.

The sheriff's steps were purposeful as he made his way across the patch of roadside grass that had turned muddy from the melting snow. And Michael, as he later would confide, was beginning to think that what had been building in his imagination since his arrival in Pullman was either everything or nothing. Either he had been chasing shadows, or what he could not bring himself to articulate—not to Maryann, not to his daughters, and certainly not to Bryan—was true.

"HOW YOU ALL DOING TODAY?" the sergeant asked. There was no edge to his voice, but Bryan could not have missed that the officer had leaned across the opened window and placed his forearm across the door.

Bryan, though, looked across at the sheriff's deputy with a face that revealed nothing. The criminal justice student no doubt knew that interrogations were never won but only lost.

Michael nodded politely toward the deputy, but also chose not to speak. Perhaps he, too, understood the value of silence. Although, more likely, he was too tense to find any words.

There was a long moment when the three men all seemed to be waiting for something definitive to happen. The steady drag of the traffic speeding along I-70 filled the void.

"License," the deputy demanded at last. His tone was brisk and impatient.

Bryan obediently obeyed. There was no panic in his movements as he retrieved the document. Sergeant Ernstes, at the same time, shared what had prompted him to stop the white car. "You were right up on that van, man. I pulled you over for tailgating."

With that revelation, both father and son seemed to exhale. In an instant, the danger of something much graver had passed. And with their shared relief, a new tempo shaped the encounter.

"Where you headed?" the deputy asked.

"We're going to get some Thai food," Bryan responded earnestly.

Michael, however, felt he should clarify his son's explanation. "Well, we're coming from WSU," he corrected.

To the Indiana deputy, the initials had no meaning. "What's WSU?" he asked. Both father and son, eager to please, attempted to remedy the confusion and in the process only added to the officer's puzzlement. Ernstes could not decide whether both of them worked at the university, or who, in fact, was the student. Or if they'd headed out from Washington State on a cross-country trip to get Thai food in Pennsylvania.

"So you're coming from Washington State University. And you're going where?" the officer reiterated.

But Michael could not leave well enough alone. Ever since he'd awoken to the news from Pullman that morning, he had been trying to make sense of the emotions roiling inside him. It had been the catalyst that gave concrete shape to the thoughts he'd been trying not to think. And now he could not hold back. He started rambling on about the shooting earlier that day at WSU.

That grabbed the officer's attention.

And Bryan's, too. The look on his face had suddenly grown cautious.

"So what did you say about some SWAT teams?" the officer asked, alert with a new interest. Michael's explanation was laborious. In his discursive way, he seemed determined to share everything except what was really front and center in his thoughts. "Interesting," the deputy remarked without apparent interest.

Michael, however, was set on having the last word. "Well, it's horrifying."

But whether he was talking about the shooting that morning or something else was never explained.

Bryan, though, must have had his suspicions. Resolved to put an end to any further march through this minefield, he spoke up. "We don't know about that actually. We weren't there for the shooting." The words bristled with indignation.

And Michael caught the familiar haughty tone, and he rushed to correct it. "We're slightly punchy because we've been driving for hours," he immediately conceded.

The deputy had had enough.

"Do me a favor," he said to Bryan. "Don't follow too closely, okay?"

And suddenly the officer was in a big hurry and then let them go without issuing a ticket.

BUT THE KOHBERGERS DO NOT get very far. Nine minutes later, Bryan once more saw flashing lights in his rearview mirror. A state trooper was ordering him to pull over.

As the white car moved to the shoulder, the Kohbergers must have had a sense that they were condemned to live out the same anxious day in a maddening reoccurrence of the same unnerving events. Or, no less a possibility, they feared that this time their luck had finally run out.

THE FBI SURVEILLANCE TEAM THAT had been assigned to tail the Kohbergers since they had left Pullman had similar thoughts. Their luck, they feared, had run out, too. There was an iron rule of law enforcement that in any long-running op the unexpected was to be expected at any time. But twice? And in such rapid succession? What were the odds?

Or maybe it had been purposeful? Had the Indiana cops figured out what the bureau was up to and wanted to rush in to make the arrest? A ragged procession of unmarked surveillance cars was scattered up and down I-70, and high in the flat blue Indiana sky a fixed-wing plane hovered. And not a single one of the many agents in this surveillance operation had any understanding of what had just happened. All they knew was that the long weeks of dogged investigation suddenly seemed headed to a disastrous conclusion. For just as they were at last moving tantalizingly close to solving the mystery, Indiana cops seemed ready to smash all their painstaking detective work to smithereens.

And the man they suspected to be the killer of the four students would have outsmarted them all.

How had it come to this?

PART III

THE HUNTER'S STORY

"Some of my young officers are gonna need your help,"
Moscow Police Chief James Fry told the department psychologist. "Actually, it's not just the young ones." *Getty*

FIFTEEN

You know how cops think. You know what they look for. You know all their tricks.

You're prepared. Well-trained. After all, you've taken the classes. Earned the degrees. You've gotten into the heads of bad guys, written "crime scripts," as your profs call them. You've learned from their mistakes.

But it's one thing to ace Advanced Crime Scene Investigations. And it's another to commit a crime. Especially when the crime is murder.

So you program a route into your phone they wouldn't expect. It'll take a bit longer, but it'll still get you where you want to go.

All you need to do is keep driving.

You were vigilant. Meticulous. Took precautions. Killing is easy. And so is getting away with it.

Nothing's changed—except they're all dead.

Afterward, when tempers were still boiling hot, fingers would be pointed at the emergency services dispatcher. She was, it was charged first by the local cops, then the state troopers, and finally the feds, responsible for the initial confusion. It was her lack of precision—or was it just nonchalance?—that had helped turn the case from the onset into such a puzzle. Her first report had failed to convey the horrific dimensions of the tragedy to the Moscow PD, and as a consequence valuable time had been lost.

A forensic squad should have arrived in lockstep with the responding police officers. The entire area should have been scoured for clues while the trail remained unblemished. The neighbors should have been questioned about what they might have seen or heard in the preceding hours while their memories were still fresh. And in the absence of a suspect, the authorities hurled their fury at the poor dispatcher.

The reality, however, was that the dispatcher had performed her job perfectly.

The town's 911 calls were routinely routed to Pullman, ten miles west across the state line in Washington, where they were handled by the civilian employees of a municipal agency called Whitcom 9–1–1. The calls came in from the local Whitman and Asotin Counties, as well as the city of Moscow, two universities with a total of about forty-two thousand students, and seventy additional municipal and county agencies. The dispatch crews, as the local newspapers were frequently documenting, were severely understaffed. It was a schedule, the overworked members of the dispatcher's guild had complained, that left "our ability to uphold public safety at risk."

And things only got busier on football weekends. As a result, when callers were agitated, rather than risk injurious delays by probing for details, the responders had been schooled to assign a generic explanation. "Unconscious person" was one of the standard catchphrases. It could mean precisely what it said, or it could be shorthand for something more ominous.

It was 11:58 a.m. on Sunday, November 13, 2022, when the notification of an "unconscious person" at a residence on 1122 King Road, Moscow, was passed on to Sergeant Shaine Gunderson. Sitting at his desk on the second floor of the sparkling new—it had opened with great ceremony barely eleven months earlier—Southview Avenue police headquarters, Gunderson was running the Operations Division.

He was midway through a twelve-hour shift that had started at 6:00 a.m., and prior to that moment, his tour had been long and slow. A typical languid Sunday morning punctuated by the sounds of the town's many church bells chiming in the wind. Truth was, Gunderson had been avidly mapping out in his mind a strategy for the eight-hour (if not easily more; things were always iffy out in the wild) trek to the summit of Mount Borah he and a friend from the University of Idaho psych department had been planning for the spring. It was Idaho's highest point, and the trail up the Southwest Ridge to the 12,662-foot summit was a steep, hard climb. And, he'd admit after a beer or two, it was just the sort of challenge he'd been missing lately.

Now that he had his sergeant's stripes, police work was more about distributing memos and filing papers than getting out into the field. That bothered him. After nearly ten years on the force, he still wanted to be the keyed-up officer who had signed on straight out of Lewis-Clark State College, in nearby Lewiston, and worked his way up to patrolman. In his early days, he'd distinguished himself as a hands-on cop, someone out in the streets doing "community policing." Back then, he'd scored a lot of points both in and out of the department (as well as winning Officer of the Year) when he single-handedly planned and organized a hot dog barbecue bringing together the cops and local schoolkids; the department put a lot of stock in that kind of genial outreach and, in fact, viewed it as the main part of the job in a small town like Moscow.

Gunderson was from the area, having grown up in Potlatch (population 774) and, still smarting from his own childhood run-ins, he knew only too well how hard-ass cops could sour things, make encounters confrontational. His job, he'd say with an earnest dedication, was "looking out for and working with the citizens of Moscow."

When the 911 call came in, Gunderson had a corporal and two other officers on duty to assist with patrol. He could have left the response to them. He certainly, he'd tell people with a hint of embarrassment, had no intimation of something out of the ordinary. That morning he was just eager to break the monotony.

He decided he'd go to the scene with his officers.

IT WAS A QUICK TRIP from headquarters. The roads leading into the university neighborhood that Sunday were as empty as the classrooms. Gunderson's black-and-white cruiser pulled up behind the orderly row of cars parked in the driveway on King Road, and he immediately knew something was very wrong.

It was the noise: there wasn't any. A cluster of young people, university students presumably, were milling outside the open front door of 1122 like gulls on a beach. Yet they were huddled in an eerie, unnatural silence. They seemed overwhelmed, shocked. When the three mystified officers approached the front door, someone in the crowd, it would later be shared, spoke a single, plaintive word: "Dead." It lingered in the cold, sharp morning air, a monosyllabic wail.

Still, Gunderson would confess to others, he was unprepared for the strong smell of blood that rose in his nostrils the moment he walked inside.

THERE ARE MOMENTS, COPS WILL tell you, that are too profound, too unnerving, to be experienced in the present. All you can do is move forward; there will be time later to make sense of it all. Procedure takes precedence. A protective membrane is stretched between the real and the too real. All other thoughts, all other feelings, become extraneous. And so Gunderson and his two officers, largely mute, almost robotic in their movements, now stepped carefully across the blood-streaked wooden floors and proceeded to inspect a crime scene. They moved cautiously, not knowing what they'd find. Yet, of course, by now they knew.

The first floor, nevertheless, was a surprise. There were two bedrooms, and when they anxiously entered each one, there was no sign out of the ordinary. They were empty, and nothing looked as if it had been disturbed.

Relieved and now hoping that their worst fears had been a wild invention, they marched single-file up the narrow stairwell to the second floor. Following the trail of deep, dark blood that sluiced across the wooden floor, they turned to the right. When they crossed into the bedroom, there were two dead bodies, a male and a female. Xana Kernodle and Ethan Chapin were gruesomely drenched in blood, yet both of their good-looking faces had, oddly, been preserved like masks.

On the other side of the second floor, adjacent to the living room, the officers had another small moment when their hopes swelled: the bedroom was empty and nothing looked out of place.

Then they climbed the stairs to the third floor and proceeded in solemn silence. At the top of the stairwell, they turned right. In the bedroom, lying in the bed that took up most of the space in the room, was the inert body of Madison Mogen. In a corner, slumped to the floor like a rag doll, was Kaylee Goncalves. The cops wondered if they were sisters, so similar were the twenty-one-year-olds' pretty, sculpted features and the long cascades of thick, streaked blond hair falling down to their narrow shoulders. A cursory examination revealed one gruesome difference: Kaylee had been hacked with a particular ferocity. It was as if her wild assailant—or was it assailants?—had been intent on gouging out chunks of her flesh. Maddie's wounds appeared less feral, more measured—at least in comparison.

Across the narrow hallway was one final door. The officers pulled it open with trepidation. And at last they discovered a sign of life: a fluffy caramel-colored dog. It was Murphy, Kaylee's goldendoodle pup. He was unharmed, not marred by even a speck of blood.

How much time had passed since the three officers had entered the house? It had only been minutes, less than a quarter of an hour according to the department's tally, but Gunderson already felt bone weary. It was a struggle to find the will to continue. He felt like throwing up his hands in surrender; the enormity of what he had seen was unlike anything he had ever experienced or could have previously imagined. For a rough moment, he felt like today would be a very good day to pack everything in and head off on his ascent of Mount Borah, winter be damned. But then, just like that, his years of discipline fell into place, and he went to work. And his first order of business was to alert his boss.

SIXTEEN

Captain Roger Lanier, the head of the twenty-four-officer Operations Division, had just taken his place at the head of the dining room table to enjoy Sunday lunch with his family when his cell phone rang. The roast was resting on the table, and he had been poised to pick up the carving knife, but he realized that if his sergeant was calling, he'd better answer. As things worked out, the captain would never get to have his lunch that day.

"It took me a second," Lanier recalled, a sharp edge even weeks later to the memory. "I really had to think about what I had just heard. Four murders in Moscow, Idaho, was so out of character."

But he knew, like every professional would, that he needed to get to work. In a murder case, delay only benefited the killer. A veteran cop, Lanier had spent more than twenty years on the force in nearby Lewiston before having been lured, six years earlier, to Moscow with a captain's rank. After all his time on the job, he'd become a steady, avuncular presence. He never got flustered because, as he'd tell people, he had seen it all in his day. Until that Sunday.

He had a thousand questions he wanted to ask Gunderson, and yet he knew the only hope of finding answers would be to follow the previously established protocols. Dutifully, he gave the order to set up the perimeters of the crime scene, to bring in the forensic team, to summon the coroner. It was standard in a major case—and if four homicides wasn't a major case, what was?—to alert the Idaho State Police, and he did that, too.

Moscow was the responsibility of the state's District 2 Detective Office in Lewiston, the county seat and where he'd been on the job for two decades. He knew many of the state detectives; still, it was a difficult conversation.

His next call didn't get easier. The university had to be informed. It was not just that four students had been brutally murdered. There was no way of knowing whether the killer—or killers—planned to strike again. The students needed to be warned and protected.

At 3:07 p.m., a distressingly long three hours after the trio of cops had entered the blood-soaked house, the University Office of Public Safety and Security sent a "Vandal Alert" email to the students and faculty: "Moscow PD investigating a homicide on King Rd. near campus. Suspect is not known at this time. Stay away from the area and shelter in place." A "shelter in place" order mandated that people "take refuge in a room with no or few windows."

At this point in the investigation, Lanier had been at the helm for hours and despite his marathon of activities, he still had no clue about a suspect, or why the murders had occurred. And, nearly just as upsetting, he had not yet been able to speak with his boss, James Fry, the chief of police.

THE CHIEF HAD BEEN GETTING death threats. There were six in all, a virulent collection of unsigned letters and barking phone messages vowing he'd be killed. And those missives were in addition to the tall pile of rude and scatological, albeit less murderous, emails and notes he had received.

The ostensible reason for the threats? He had ordered his officers to enforce the mayor's and the city council's coronavirus restrictions.

People had received summonses for not wearing masks in public. Then at a defiantly maskless prayer vigil in the city hall parking lot, several of the more reverent in the open-air assembly had been cuffed and hauled off on Fry's orders. His no-nonsense policing had made the chief a lot of enemies.

The municipal restriction ran counter to the libertarian spirit of many Idahoans. And Pastor Doug Wilson had added fuel to this fire. He had told his Christ Church parishioners that masks and vaccinations were counter to "God's teachings." But by the fateful November weekend when the murders occurred, Chief Fry had hoped that all the bad feelings that'd been simmering in the town over the past two years had, with the end of the pandemic controls, also largely slipped away. It was now a time of reconciliation; the Kirkers would even send the department Christmas cookies. (Yet when the chief thanked them on Facebook, several of the town's die-hard liberals wrote a letter to the local paper fuming that he was kowtowing to the church group.)

The previous spring, Fry had passed on his chance to go on a prolonged elk hunt; he hadn't felt right about leaving Moscow for too long. But he no longer had such qualms that fall. On November 12, Fry and his wife, Julie, had driven off to spend the weekend at a friend's home nearly three hours away.

By the time Lanier had finally reached the chief, it was hours after the discovery of the bodies. And when Fry finally entered the home on King Road, it was dark outside—according to several dismayed accounts, close to 6:00 p.m. For some abstruse reason, he'd thought it important to go home first and change into his chief's uniform. Possibly he hadn't fully grasped the magnitude of the disaster. Or maybe, after nearly twenty-eight years as a Moscow cop, he felt the imprimatur of his uniform was integral to his ability to command.

What he saw that evening, he'd publicly say, "was the worst crime scene I'd ever seen." To a friend, he'd be more revelatory: walking through the blood-drenched house had left him "physically and emotionally drained." He was a father of two daughters who had attended the University of Idaho, and he himself had graduated from the university nearly three decades earlier. It was impossible, he said, not to feel a visceral tie to the victims and to their parents.

His mind was racing as he exited the murder house. He did not know how to begin to make sense of what he had just seen. He needed to find a path forward.

THREE YEARS EARLIER, FRY HAD been chosen to attend the ten-week course at the FBI's National Academy in Quantico, Virginia. He was on the cusp of turning fifty, and the impending milestone, he'd confided to a close friend, had triggered a soul-searching. He'd wanted to prove that even as he was acknowledging the inevitability of his soon becoming a senior citizen, he was still the sort of cop who could break up a bar fight or strap on SWAT gear when some local went berserk and started shooting up the courthouse. A chief went to lunches at the Chamber of Commerce and played golf with the mayor. Fry wanted to show that in spite of his title, he had remained a cop's cop. His friends called him "old-school," and it was an appraisal that had always sat well with him.

It had, therefore, been very important to Fry to complete the 6.1-mile obstacle course at Quantico called "the Yellow Brick Road." The signs nailed to the tree at the starting line read HURT, AGONY, and PAIN. There was climbing over walls, crawling under barbed wire, sloshing through streams, hauling up steep cliffs, and running full speed through rocky, winding trails. It was an unforgiving ordeal.

And Fry did it. The certificate he'd received in recognition of this accomplishment was displayed with pride across from his desk in headquarters.

But on that deeply perturbing evening in November he recalled another memory. A day or so before he'd taken on the Yellow Brick Road, he'd been to a class led by a member of the FBI Behavioral Science Unit.

The lecturer had explained how the bureau had been able to get into the heads of killers. They had studied what made them kill, and how to catch them before they would kill again.

What if, Fry asked himself with sudden alarm, a serial killer had attacked the four students? What if it was only a matter of time before this maniac struck again? The entire Moscow PD was just thirty-seven officers, and he doubted that any of them had the expertise to handle the strange and unfamiliar places where, if his worst fears proved accurate, the hunt would take them.

Shaken by this thought, Chief Fry called the bureau and asked for their assistance. It was quickly arranged. A team of special agents, eventually about forty in total, would be arriving as soon as tomorrow. And as he had specifically requested, three members of the Behavioral Analysis Unit, two men and a woman, were also being dispatched.

Yet Fry was still not done, and now with the dawn of the new day, he realized there was something important he'd forgotten.

WHEN RAND WALKER GOT THE call, he was in his GMC pickup heading down the twisting seven-hundred-foot driveway that led from his house to the main road into town. He looked at the caller ID and figured he knew why the chief was calling first thing in the morning. His friend wanted to apologize.

A week or so earlier, Walker along with his band had been playing downtown at Bucer's Coffeehouse & Pub. They performed '70s cover songs—a lot of Eagles, a lot of Van Morrison, and their version of Neil Diamond's "Sweet Caroline" was a get-out-of-your-seat showstopper. They had quite a die-hard following in northern Idaho. And the chief had promised to be there, only he never showed.

"No problem, Chief," Walker began breezily. "I know you got plenty to do. You'll catch us next time."

"It's something else," Fry said curtly. "I need you to stand by."

At once Walker understood that something awful had happened.

A PhD with a private practice in Moscow, he also served as the department's psychologist.

"Some of my young officers are gonna need your help," Fry continued. Then he corrected himself. "Actually, it's not just the young ones."

IT WAS SURPRISING, THEN, THAT, despite the raw fears that had been shared with the FBI, the police department issued a series of statements deliberately crafted to reassure the public. On the same seemingly hopeless day when he first toured the crime scene, the official party line announced, "The Moscow Police does not believe there is an ongoing community risk based on information gathered during the preliminary investigation." Then two days later, the department doubled down on this: "We determined early in the investigation that we do not believe there is an ongoing threat for community members. Evidence indicates that this was a targeted attack."

Fry and his department, however, had no idea whether the community was at risk, or whether the killer might strike again on campus or elsewhere in town.

In his defense, perhaps Fry had come to believe that his lack of candor was a small sin when measured against the panic that would spread through campus and the town if he shared his uncertainty. That it was, in truth, anybody's guess whether the killer would return and the body count of young students would increase.

Or, no less plausible, perhaps after staring at the red blood that had seeped through the floor of the murder house and had run down the building's gray concrete foundation like crimson lightning bolts, he needed to believe that such a thing would not happen again. It was as much a comfort to himself as to anyone else.

SEVENTEEN

From the start they went into battle. Every morning promptly at 7:00 a.m. the newly assembled taskforce met for a daily briefing in the conference room in police headquarters. Even the FBI agents, who had set up their own base in a blue trailer parked in the headquarters parking lot, came. The conference room was big, filled with rows of polished blond wood tables sitting on a gray patterned carpet. Ceiling lights kept things very bright, and there was a band of small rectangular windows running in a row near the top of a side wall that let in light, too. Everything looked brand-new, almost corporate, as if a midlevel insurance company had just moved in. But there was a murder board adjacent to a far wall with rows of gruesome homicide photos, and everyone in the room had a gun.

Standing at the front room leading the briefings each morning, taking charge, was a young Moscow police corporal, Brett Payne.

THE WOLF HAD GOTTEN AWAY. It was spring break 2010, and Brett Payne, a twenty-year-old University of Idaho student, had been determined to bag the big gray wolf that had been seen roaming up on Lindstrom Peak deep in the high timber of northern Idaho's St. Joe National Forest. After four days, Payne hadn't found a single paw print.

When Payne broke camp that morning, he considered giving up, but the prospect of leaving the mountain empty-handed just didn't feel right. So he kept at it, and about 4:00 p.m., the sun still high in the sky, he spotted tracks. He followed them for the next two hours.

And there it was: a big male wolf lying across a draw in the middle of the road, about three hundred yards in the distance.

Carefully, with the utmost quiet, Payne lowered himself to the forest floor. He could see the animal clearly through his rifle scope. If the wolf caught a human scent, he'd bolt. But the wind was in Payne's favor.

He put his finger on the rifle's trigger, started to apply pressure, yet still hesitated. "It was intense," he later explained. He needed to calm down.

But suddenly the wolf raised his head, so Payne shot. The bullet went through the animal's chest, dropping it at once. Payne had bagged his wolf.

It was now twelve years later, and Payne was once again the relentless hunter. Only now he was on the trail of a different sort of predator—a mass murderer. Payne had come to the Moscow PD just two years earlier, after serving in the no-nonsense 82nd Airborne in Afghanistan; he had been in some very difficult situations—"touch-and-go" was all he'd say to anyone who asked, refusing to give details. Then he'd done a stint stateside in the MPs, and that, too, required that a soldier knew how to handle himself. Chief Fry had taken an instant liking to his confident, squared-away military demeanor, and promoted him quickly to corporal over other, more experienced officers. When the state police had asked who'd be leading the morning briefings, Fry, without thinking too much about it, chose Payne.

The chief knew that Payne, although new to the force, had been involved in several complex forensic investigations with the MPs. That sort of technical expertise, the chief suspected, could come in handy. And Fry had heard the story about the wolf. The chief, an old elk hunter himself, had come to appreciate that tenacity was half the battle, maybe more, in any hunt.

———

IN THOSE FIRST, TENTATIVE DAYS, it was the taskforce's operating conviction that there had to be a logic to the crime, and through meticulous probing it would be revealed. Once they understood why the murders had happened, then the path to identifying the killer would be made clear. And so the base from which they launched their attack was two-pronged. They divided their inquiries into the empirical and the theoretical.

The empirical side of the ledger listed the facts.

Fact: The four students were killed in their sleep, sometime between 3:00 and 5:00 a.m. (In the weeks ahead, they'd develop a more precise timeline: the murders, the authorities deduced, occurred between around 4:00 and 4:20 in the morning.)

Fact: There was no sign of forced entry, or of robbery, or of sexual assault.

Fact: There was no trail of blood outside the house.

Fact: The King Road residence, a well-visited party house in the months before the murders, was a repository for a large collection of forensic evidence—blood, saliva, hair, fingerprints, DNA. Within two weeks of the murders, the investigators had, they announced, collected 103 pieces of individual evidence, catalogued approximately four thousand photographs of the crime scene, and conducted multiple 3D scans of the house. Yet a more disturbing truth, and one they worked to suppress, was that so far they had nothing substantive to show for all this effort.

Fact: It had been determined that a single weapon had been used—a long-bladed knife.

And a corollary to that was a substantial secret the investigators were not yet ready to reveal: In the third-floor bedroom, tangled in the sheets next to Maddie's sprawled body, they had found a knife sheath with a button snap. It was tan leather, stamped with the brand name KA-BAR and below that USMC and the Marine Corps eagle, globe, and anchor insignia. It was a widely available weapon, sold online and in sporting goods stores, and used by sportsmen, hunters, the military, and, apparently, the killer.

Fact—and this, too, was another item they were deliberately keeping locked away: they had an eyewitness. Dylan Mortensen had seen the murderer. And, even more promising, she'd been able to give a broad yet nevertheless cogent description of the masked, black-clad intruder, down to his bushy eyebrows.

However, this quite possibly crucial eyewitness came with a lot of baggage that, the team conceded among themselves, left them dumbfounded. She had, alerted by the early morning suspicious noise, poked her head out of her second-floor bedroom three (!) separate times as her roommates were being hacked to death. She had seen a masked intruder, stared at him, "frozen" and in "shock," immobile, never uttering a word or a scream before closing the door to her bedroom and retreating to the safety of her bed. And yet during the course of that long, terrible night, she had never once picked up her cell phone to call 911. A further troubling mystery: she had waited until around 11:00 that morning—seven endless hours!—before telling anyone that things were amiss. Then, bewilderingly, she reached out with a vague call of alarm to friends, summoning them to the house. It was one of Ethan's golfing buddies, Hunter Johnson, who just moments after taking one quick look inside the house, grabbed Dylan's cell phone and, his voice a shriek, called 911.

The investigators did not know what to make of Dylan's behavior. Shock can send people careening down strange paths, they realized. But the enormity of her disconnection, her long hours of passivity, threw them for a loop.

Then, after having grappled with the facts, the team each morning would turn to the still-theoretical aspects of the investigation. And here the search for truth was more tenuous: the best they could come up with were hypotheses, and those, as any veteran detective knew, were a dime a dozen, and still you'd be overpaying. Yet since the crime made no sense, how could they in good faith rule out any theory, no matter how seemingly preposterous?

Finally, at the end of each of the morning sessions in the opening days of the hunt, the team would take a long, hard look at what remained unknown. They couldn't figure out how the killer had gotten away without apparently leaving a clue. They had no idea where the murder weapon might be. And they had not the slightest understanding of why he had chosen these victims.

IT WAS ARTHUR CONAN DOYLE back in 1887 who first introduced the role of a "consulting detective." "Here in London," Doyle's masterful hero Sherlock Holmes boasted, "we have lots of Government detectives and lots of private ones. When the fellows are at fault they come to me, and I manage to put them on the right scent."

And as the investigation in Moscow plodded on and frustratingly on without significant result, Chief Fry decided that what had worked for Sherlock Holmes could work for him, too. He called out for help, appealing to locals to become, in effect, "consulting detectives." He wanted help to put his men "on the right scent."

"Detectives are looking for context to the events and people involved in these murders," a Moscow PD press release announced. "To assist with the ongoing investigation, any odd or out-of-the-ordinary events that took place should be reported." The notice urged, "Your information, whether you believe it significant or not, might be the piece of the puzzle that helps investigators solve these murders."

And so the tips poured in. It was, after all, never easier to be a sleuth. A new generation of consulting detectives armed with cell phones and laptops, with ready access to a vast repository of information about the victims, from selfies and Instagram and Facebook posts, embraced the opportunity.

It wouldn't be long before more than 20,000 tips were received. That catalogue of suspicions included more than 9,025 emails, 4,575 phone calls to the hotline, and 6,050 digital-media submissions. An army of law-enforcement analysts was assigned to sift through the collection. It was the back bearing of all time, and much of it led down rabbit holes of fatuous speculation.

Some of the "clues" were not just wrongheaded but cruel. Innocent ex-boyfriends; the hoodie-wearing bystander at the late-night food truck; a garrulous King Road neighbor who insisted on sharing rambling half-baked anecdotes with every reporter who knocked on his door; and frat brothers who were rumored to be stoked up on steroids and driven by long-gestating grievances—all were persistently slandered with a malicious authority. It got so crazy that a history prof at the university decided that she had to sue to put an end to one Internet sleuth's bizarre speculation—it had come to her in a psychic vision—that a failed romance with one of the female victims had driven the teacher to kill.

Yet in the end, all the shaking of the trees had amounted to nothing. And Fry now realized he had to retreat from his earlier professed certitude. At a press conference, the chief quietly conceded that he could not confirm there was no ongoing threat to the community. Residents should, he said with a defeated resignation, "remain vigilant."

EIGHTEEN

———

As the days passed and the case dragged on inconclusively, Steve Goncalves struggled to make sense of his emotions. In the agonized aftermath of his daughter Kaylee's murder, Steve, his wife, and their remaining children had been brought low. But more demonstratively than the others in the family, his anger, as displayed in his public utterances, spewed out raw and unfettered. One day he railed with an uncomprehending anguish at the injustice of it all. "You can't imagine sending your girl to college and they come back . . . in an urn," he grieved openly to a group of reporters. "You're numb . . . you can't absorb that amount of pain and agony." Next he chose to scorn the capricious, faltering manner with which, he had decided, law enforcement had been attempting to solve the murders. "I do not feel confident," he responded with a vehement candor, when asked on a news show what he thought about the police investigation. "And that's why I push the envelope and say a little more."

Yet even as he made himself available to nearly every journalist who reached out to him, Steve couldn't help feeling, he confided to a friend, that all his heartfelt proclamations, everything he had been calling truths, added up to little more than a sort of self-indulgence. His public sharing of his anguish and misgivings gave him little comfort. "I hate to be that guy," he would say.

More disheartening, after all his years as a father, of devoting himself full-time to what he thought best for his children, he was confronted with the devastating reality that there was nothing more he could do for Kaylee. And, hand in hand with that, another sorrow: he couldn't identify a clear-headed strategy to lead his grieving family forward. Never had he been so unprepared, and yet never had his family needed him so much. He was at a loss.

For weeks he had been struggling. No dogma, only emotions. It was as if he'd been letting himself be tossed around by the surging waves of breaking news. But now finally he knew what he would do.

He would do it because for a father no sacrifice is too great. And a father's duty to his child never ends, not even with her death.

He would do it because while he was a man alone, with his family's support and assistance, they became a force whose commitment and focus was greater than anything the so-called authorities could muster.

He would do it because to walk any other path would be weakness, or even cowardice.

He would join the hunters. He would solve the case.

And he would do it because it was what his beloved Kay-Kay would have done—and had, in fact, tried to do.

OCTOBER 5, 2021, HAD BEEN a surprisingly cool Tuesday in Moscow, a day when the sudden drop in temperature was the first unwanted reminder that a glorious Indian summer was over and the northwest winter would soon be closing in.

Yet undeterred by the chill, as soon as she'd finished her last class, Kaylee convinced her boyfriend, Jack DuCoeur, to accompany her to the Walmart Supercenter on Pullman Road. The warehouse store was vast and unattractive, sitting atop acres of black asphalt parking lanes like a stolid concrete fortress. But it had a lot of stuff; you could find pretty much anything. And Kaylee loved to shop.

The two students had been wandering through the maze of harshly lit aisles when Kaylee first noticed the grandmotherly woman. She had pale, stringy hair and the bewildered look of someone trapped in a situation she couldn't quite understand. But more unnerving was the animal straightness of the woman's stare. She fixed her gaze on Kaylee and held it, way past anything that could be considered polite, or for that matter, normal. It wasn't threatening, but nevertheless it was decidedly odd.

Then, when Kaylee and Jack were at the checkout counter, she happened to look up absently, only to discover that the woman, now standing at rigid attention with her back to a wall of shelves, had once again homed in on her with the same unremitting stare. It was creepy. What was up with her? Kaylee wondered.

Hours later she knew. She had just seen the face again, this time on a missing persons flyer. The woman, Kaylee was convinced, was Sharon Archer, a frail sixty-two-year-old suffering from acute diabetes and brain damage who had abruptly vanished a week earlier from the house she shared with her husband up north in Coeur d'Alene. The couple's car, a 2013 white Toyota Highlander, was missing, too. No one knew what had happened, and in the absence of real information, increasingly feverish Internet speculations flourished. The scenarios ran the gamut from a mental breakdown to more fanciful schemes involving abduction or murder.

But now Kaylee knew. And at 10:25 that night, just moments after all the pieces had clicked into place in her mind, Kaylee promptly telephoned the Moscow Police Department. She spoke to Sergeant Dustin Blaker, telling him she was convinced she'd spotted the woman, and then, for good measure, she sent an email with the missing persons notice attached.

Despite the late hour, the sergeant, a barrel-chested weightlifter with just over a year on the force, conscientiously went to work. Officers were dispatched to the Walmart parking lot, and they combed the dark recesses for a telltale Toyota. At the same time, calls were made to local hotels asking if a woman matching Sharon Archer's description had checked in. Both searches were futile. And accessing the Walmart surveillance camera videos proved to be problematic: it had to be postponed until the next day, and then it, too, turned out to be another dead end.

As it happened, it wasn't Kaylee's call that solved the mystery. More than two anxious weeks passed before an angler perched on a dock noticed a bulky shape entombed in the lead-gray depths of Fernan Lake, a popular fishing spot about a ten-minute drive from downtown Coeur d'Alene. When police lifted a white Toyota Highlander from the water, a body lay inside. The autopsy identified the corpse as Sharon Archer, and while the specific circumstances of her grim death remain conjectural, no foul play has ever been charged. The investigation petered out, soon to be overtaken by fresh tragedies.

ONLY NOW STEVE FOUND HIMSELF recalling his daughter's attempt to solve that mystery. And it had dawned on him that just as Kaylee had unhesitatingly thrown herself into the investigation, he had a responsibility, too. He was caught up in a true-crime story, and prodded by his daughter's example, he would act. He would play the detective.

Sweeping all the extraneous emotional debris cluttering his mind aside, deciding to live by his wits, he went on the hunt. Working with Alivea, his oldest daughter, Steve began checking out Kaylee's phone for clues. The two of them went through the list of contacts, reached out to Kaylee's friends, and helped to reconstruct the last hours of his daughter's and her best friend Maddie's last hours and shared them with the authorities.

They also discovered the persistent series of calls in the wee hours of the morning from Kaylee to her ex-boyfriend, Jack DuCoeur—calls that had gone unanswered. Steve quickly passed that intelligence, too, on to the cops.

When the Moscow PD summarily hooked Jack up to a lie detector and administered a DNA swab to compare with evidence at the crime scene, he passed both examinations, according to one of Steve's friends.

Steve, however, was not completely assuaged. Nothing about the murders made any sense, and so everything seemed possible. Suspicions lay claim to his thoughts.

When a grieving Jack came to the Goncalveses' home not long after the events to pay his respects, Steve gravely demanded that the young man submit to the indignity of a physical inspection. Jack promptly rolled up his sleeves, lifted his shirt, exposed his neck, displayed his hands, palms up and down, while Steve meticulously searched in vain for a telltale scratch or bruise.

But Steve was not done. Caught up in his newfound forensic professionalism, he took a series of photographs documenting Jack's unblemished state. It was exculpatory evidence that would come in handy, he felt, as the authorities proceeded to compile their list of suspects. And with that bit of awkward business out of the way, the two grieving men finally embraced.

In the days that followed, Steve tracked down Hunter Johnson, Chapin's close friend. Just before noon on November 13, Johnson—incredibly, prior to even the police having been notified—had been summoned by the two distraught survivors to the King Road house. He had discovered Ethan's body. And now he gave his eyewitness account to Steve as a soldier might: straightforward, factual, and without embellishment or emotion. It was only when he finished that the two men, both overwhelmed, at last convulsed into tears.

Steve also made a point of knocking on the doors of the houses adjacent to the murder scene and interrogating neighbors. And he had posted on Facebook, asking if anyone had any information. He was going where he felt he had to go, but his mission had not produced the desired results. Weeks had passed, and there had been no arrests. The authorities had not even named a suspect. It was infuriating. The prospect of his daughter's murder becoming one more cold case was a torture.

But as much as he needed to see a perp being led off in handcuffs, he was also chasing after something else. He needed to know: Why?

Why these kids? Why this house? Why had this nightmare enveloped his family's life? For his own peace of mind, he required a motive. And without this knowledge, nothing in his life from November 13 onward would ever make sense.

It was, he'd let people know, those currents of frustration and perplexity that pushed him to double down on his detective's mission. He made up his mind to reach out to more people and to proclaim his new, ambitious vocation more directly. He would make a public appeal. Steve was certain that even if the police had failed to locate them, there had to be people out there who knew more than they were sharing. Someone, particularly a student with some dodgy antics to hide, might be more willing to whisper secrets to a mourning father than to the judgmental police.

With this plan in mind, Steve reached out to Olivia Vitale.

NINETEEN

———

To listen to Olivia Vitale tell it, she had never paid much attention to how her father earned his living. The fact that he'd been a hard-driving crime reporter in his native Chicago and then had gone on to a career as both a reporter and editor in Los Angeles had not made much of an impression on her when she was growing up in Washington State. Her parents had divorced, and her dad's occupation in a distant city was an irrelevancy.

Or so she had thought. For as a precocious twenty-two-year-old working in real estate in Florida, Vitale had been inexplicably drawn to the flurry of stories in the media recounting the brutal murder of Gabby Petito by her fiancé as the freewheeling young couple had vanned across the country.

Not constrained by any formal journalistic training or experience, Olivia posted personal, empathetic, yet carefully researched videos about the case on TikTok and YouTube. And she didn't stop posting when this mystery was put to rest and had vanished from the front pages.

Inventive and persistent, Vitale hitched a ride on the comet tail of the zooming true-crime business. She chased one confounding case after another. Within a year or so, "The Chronicles of Olivia" was pulling in tens of millions of viewers. By the time she was twenty-five, Vitale was one of the go-to sources for a generation who got their crime stories—down, dirty, and dishy—from the Internet. And one of her avid followers had been Kaylee.

Steve had discovered this connection when he had been checking out Kaylee's phone for clues. And it got him thinking.

OLIVIA ASSUMED IT WAS A hoax, one more Internet fabrication. She did not believe that Kaylee's dad had actually contacted her. And so she didn't respond.

But the email kept nagging at her. Was it possible it had been sent by Steve Goncalves? And if so, she could be on the verge of a scoop. With a diligence that belied her twenty-five years, she tracked down Alivea Goncalves, who confirmed that it was in fact her father's email address. Excited, Olivia wrote back.

It was a pragmatically brief courtship; both would benefit from the Goncalveses' appearance on "The Chronicles of Olivia." And more serendipity—Olivia, hot on the case from the onset, was already in Moscow. It'd be just ninety minutes straight up US-95 North to the Goncalveses' home. The meeting was quickly arranged.

Vitale was filled with trepidation as she and her producer, "Bullhorn Betty" (that was her "nom de Internet") set up inside the family's daffodil-yellow living room for the interview with Steve, Kristi, and Alivea. Without any network imprimatur, Vitale had landed the sort of scoop that, a generation earlier, would have gone to Barbara Walters. But the Idaho murders was a news story owned by a new breed of journalists, an event sustained by the nonstop fulsome attention it received on the Internet.

And for the citizen reporters, it was a burgeoning, often very profitable business. YouTube segments produced by intrepid social media journalists who had scurried to Moscow to film events on their cell phones or DSLR cameras were routinely followed by appeals. "Don't forget to like, share, and subscribe. Please consider making a donation to PayPal,

CashApp, or Venmo." "Printing money" was how Bullhorn Betty had described the lucrative success of the various YouTube segments she had independently posted online before she had joined up with Olivia.

So perhaps it was unsurprising that the stakes—money as well as celebrity—fueled resentment. The sense of injury over someone's getting more likes, of racking up more subscribers, made the internecine Internet squabbles a nasty, sneeringly competitive business.

Sydney Norton, as Brat Norton on TikTok and YouTube, had succeeded, without leaving her home in North Carolina, in landing a series of scoops: access to family members of the victims and, impressively, probing interviews with authorities involved in the case. A glamorous thirty-two-year-old, she also had star power; she was getting a lot of attention. As a consequence, perhaps it was inevitable that one of her envious Internet competitors decided to take her down a peg.

Norton received an incredible video. It had been recorded by a King Road neighbor, and it revealed the "real" story of what had happened that night. The neighbor, in fact, had witnessed the events from a distance. The tape, however, just laid the groundwork for the next part of the exclusive. There was an overwrought barrage of late-night calls to Norton, each an emotionally charged plea, each filled with a rising level of hysteria, the caller wailing that her secret tape and her secret knowledge had made her "a target." "I'm not safe," she pleaded to Norton. "Help me!"

Norton, caught up in the drama, convinced that her source's fear was genuine and that she was sitting on a colossal scoop, reached out to the FBI and to the authorities in Idaho. In the process, the case became no longer an abstraction, a distant news story. Its terror was now her terror. Norton grew to believe that her access to this secret knowledge had put her own life, as well as that of her young son, in jeopardy. Dangerous events were closing in on her. But in time, the videotape, while artful in its re-creation, even ingenious, was revealed as a clever fake. The hoaxer's vindictive plan: once Norton had gone public with her scoop, the embarrassing reality would've been revealed, and Norton would be discredited.

But Olivia did not have such problems. The envious competitors who had gone after Norton would not be able to impugn her work. For she was staring at the real thing—a genuine scoop.

THE GONCALVESES SIT SHOULDER TO shoulder on the couch in their living room. Vitale, who has positioned herself off camera, is a polite, disembodied voice asking the questions. But there's a hesitancy to her probing; it's as if she's acknowledging that she's intruding, that she doesn't belong in this house of grief. And her reaction is understandable. Steve's face is grim, solemn, and expressionless—as blank and flat as an empty piece of paper. Watching the tape of the interview, one can feel the harsh tension in the room. Will the Goncalveses reconsider and order Vitale and her producer to turn off the cameras?

Then something remarkable happens. The Goncalveses seem to surrender, perhaps accepting the absurdity of the situation, of their sitting in the living room talking to a stranger young enough to be one of their children about their innermost feelings with a video camera aimed at them like a weapon. A restraining wall comes tumbling down. And like all mourners, they begin to talk about the past. The heartfelt memories of Kaylee pour out.

Yet Steve recovers. He has not forgotten his agenda, and he is soon back in the present. He wants to let the ineffectual authorities know what they can expect from him. He wants them to understand that if they can't get the job done, then he will.

Staring into the camera, he proclaims with an earnest passion, "We are not going to bed and wait for other people to solve a family problem. This is a family problem." He continues to drive home the point that he's on the case: "We are not going to sit here and let someone else do a job that we can add value to." He determined, as he puts it, "to make an impact," to "listen to what people are saying," to be "a part of solving it." He needs to feel, he volunteers with an affecting candor, that "I gave it my all. I did everything that I could."

He also acknowledges his limitations, his inability to have an insider's knowledge of the furtive currents swirling through Moscow in the weeks preceding the murders. He openly appeals for help in his hunt to find the killers. "This takes a whole community. It takes all of us to solve."

The camera has now become his ally. He's staring full-faced at it, focusing directly at his audience. "This is on us," Steve declares. "Are we going to let these people exist?" And then it's as if the entire hour-long interview has built to his uttering a single terse, yet unflinching pronouncement. With his face as somber as a graveside mourner's, he promises: "I'm telling you right now, we're coming for you."

It is as much a warning to the killer as it is an ineluctable vow to himself.

PART IV

THE FORENSIC SCIENTISTS' STORY

FBI Academy in Quantico, VA. The bureau's techies hoped that science would provide the clues that would solve the case—and lead to a suspect. *U.S. Federal Government / Public Domain*

TWENTY

———

So you screwed up. You left the knife sheath behind. On the bed. Next to one of the blond girls. Sloppy.

What did that boxer say? All plans go out the window once you're punched in the mouth. Seems that's true for killing, too. Once the knife's plunged deep into flesh. Once the blood starts gushing.

But it's not a catastrophe. You know what the science can prove. And what it can't.

Science is smart. But you're smarter.

It was a time for clutching at straws. For heading off in all directions. In a case where nothing seemed to make sense, there were no guardrails. Any answer seemed as logical as another. With the national media converging on Moscow and screaming for a solution, with the grieving father of one of the victims constantly voicing his dismay at the lack of progress, a besieged Chief Fry instructed Payne to send out the team to chase down all leads.

Armed with their broad marching orders, the investigators went to work. They focused on the classmates of the female victims—boyfriends, ex-boyfriends, frat brothers, even guys the three women had casually run into on their last night out and about—and every single alibi checked out.

Still not convinced, Fry ordered they examine those stories again. Only when this second confirmation proved accurate was he at last willing to let the team move on.

Yet even as they were still heading down this long, unproductive route, an indignant female FBI agent had dangled another possibility. It was sexist, as well as bad detective work, she argued, to train our attention solely on men. Women kill, too, she pointed out with a well-documented reason. Why not a jealous sorority sister or an ex-bestie? And despite her obvious embarrassment, she shared an eye-opening tale from her own college days that proved her point about the fury of a woman scorned.

Convinced, a small group of investigators began poking into the sororities to dig up provocative dirt. Only once again, none of it had any operational relevance. But then, widening the aperture even further, they began to look at not only coeds, but women in the region who had been previously charged with assault. And just like that, they had something: a woman from up north with a history of violence who had come down to spend the football weekend in Moscow. Had one of the young female victims, or perhaps Ethan, done something to provoke her ire? But try as they might, they couldn't make the pieces fit into the puzzle. There was no intersection point between this suspect and any of the victims.

Increasingly desperate, the team's approach turned particularly scattershot; the inquiries owed as much to wishful thinking as to insightful detective work. Although there was no evidence of sexual assault to the victims, a great deal of time was spent tracing the whereabouts on November 13 of dozens of sex offenders in both Idaho and Washington State. At the same time, the rants of a loony white supremacist who lived in a nearby town caught their attention, too, and on Fry's orders they exhaustively tracked his activities on the fateful weekend. They also looked into a man who lived in an adjoining state who, a year or more earlier, had sent harassing messages to a local woman. When it was quickly determined that he had only been in Idaho twice in his life, and neither occasion was within the past six months, Fry was not deterred. Keep at it, he ordered.

Similarly, the comings and goings of a local who had once been accused of a knife attack were plotted, and then plotted again for good measure. And at their conclusions, every one of these inquiries inexorably led to very dead ends.

Payne grew tarnished and gloomy, no longer the swaggering ex-MP. Fry, desperate to keeping his team's morale from flagging, would resort to pep talks and bromides that, to the more experienced state troopers and federal agents, were quickly growing tedious. "We'll get a break, you'll see," he cheered on. "You never know when it will happen." To which one fed-up trooper, albeit when out of earshot, had sneered, "You're right. *You* never will know."

But as Fry had predicted, just when the team least expected it, they caught a break. Only problem was, they didn't realize it.

FIVE DAYS AFTER THE MURDERS, the Moscow PD issued still another request for help, but the specificity in this appeal gave it more bite:

"Moscow detectives are seeking help from residents and businesses within the area [of the King Road house] . . . who have video surveillance at their residence or business between 3 a.m. to 6 a.m. on Sunday, November 13, 2022."

The overnight assistant manager (her name, at her request, remains secret) for a gas station on Troy Road, not far from the house on King Road, read this notice and swiftly decided to help. This was her town, and a killer was on the loose, and so she felt she had a duty. She had not been working the night of the murders, but nevertheless she spent the downtime on her graveyard shift reviewing the videos that had been recorded by the station's surveillance cameras on November 13. "I had a weird feeling," she later said.

Over the course of a long night, she intermittently kept at it. It was painstaking work, and at first she found nothing. Then just before she was to wrap up her shift, the shadowy video revealed a small treasure: she spotted a white car speeding down Highway 8 before turning down a side street. The time was close to 4:30 a.m., and that was very much in the window the detectives were exploring. She took a screenshot of the footage and emailed it to the tip-line address.

Later that day, a Moscow police officer appeared at the gas station to confiscate hours of surveillance footage. The quality of the images was taxing. They were flickering, recorded in varying light. At first glance, all that could be said for sure was that the pixels had captured a fast-moving white car.

But it was a puzzle that held their attention. They kept at it. And in the end, they had something. Sure, they were unable to penetrate through the dark shadows enveloping the car's windshield to make out the face behind the wheel. And the license plate was out of the camera's shot. Nevertheless, on November 19 the team had made an important deduction: the killer had fled in a 2019–2023 white Nissan Sentra.

Armed at last with what they felt confident was a propitious lead, they once again charged off. Only they were headed in the wrong direction: the identification of the vehicle had been wrong.

INSPIRED BY THE SERVICE STATION video, an industrious detective reached out on a hunch to Kane Francetich. Recently retired, Francetich was now investing in real estate. As part of his portfolio he owned a six-unit rental complex on Linda Lane, about three-tenths of a mile from where the bodies had been found. And there was a surveillance camera fixed to the building's roof.

Francetich was a friendly, easygoing guy, eager to cooperate. "I downloaded [the rooftop camera] and gave them access to everything from 2:00 am through noon on that Sunday the thirteenth," he said.

The tapes reconfirmed a good deal of what the investigators had first seen on the gas station video. There it was—the same white car. And once again it appeared to be making a breakneck getaway through the dark King Road neighborhood streets at about 4:20 a.m.

But they now realized they had a problem: they were no longer so sure the vehicle was a Nissan. From this new angle, it certainly didn't look like one. And after a while, they conceded they were stumped. They were unable to determine the model of the car. And without any idea of the make of the car, its year, or, for that matter, its license plate number or a look at the driver, they were back at square one.

TWENTY-ONE

Building 27958-A was a stark, modernistic six-story sandstone and glass structure tucked away in a corner of the rolling, pastoral campus of the FBI training academy in Quantico, Virginia. And in Pod E, a small, harshly lit room hidden in the building's maze of offices, the forensic examiners of the FBI Operational Technology Division toiled away. Their job was to help the bureau and other government agencies determine the make, model, and year of a vehicle when there wasn't too much to work with.

To accomplish this, the examiners employed an inventive bit of software that had been originally developed (at the cost of about $1 million in taxpayer dollars) for a secretive Defense Department—the Irregular Warfare Technical Support Directorate. With the click of a series of computer keys, the program searches with a methodic diligence through a staggering inventory of cars until it "identifies the make and model of a vehicle in a still image."

Prodded by the federal agents working with the team, the stymied Moscow detectives sent copies of their collection of car videos to the forensic specialists at the Quantico-based unit. And right away, the expensive software worked like a charm. Or, more precisely, three charms. The FBI forensic examiners first deduced that Suspect Vehicle 1—the white car caught on multiple cameras leaving the crime scene—was a 2011–2013 Hyundai Elantra. However, "upon further review," they would later decide the mysterious Hyundai might very well be a 2011–2016 vehicle. Then, with the passage of even more time, as the examiners continued to pore over an additional image of a car "consistent with" the Hyundai near the murder scene, they definitively narrowed down their analysis: it was a 2014–2016.

And that was the best analysts could do. In all the inventive manipulation of the pixels in the video footage of Suspect Vehicle 1, the bureau's techies still couldn't come up with a legible shot of the license plate. Nor was there a single legible image of the driver. All they could decipher was a dark, murky shadow hovering over the steering wheel.

Another large obstacle: there were twenty-two thousand Hyundais in the region that matched the search criteria. The hunt would be a nearly impossible task, a needle-in-a-haystack sort of challenge. But what choice did they have? One of the twenty-two thousand Hyundais had very likely been driven by a killer.

On November 25, twelve days after the murders, the Moscow PD issued a nationwide "Be on the Lookout" alert, a BOLO in cop-speak. It was judiciously worded, the authorities trying not to oversell what they had:

"Detectives are interested in speaking with the occupant(s) of a white 2011–2013 Hyundai Elantra with an unknown license plate . . . Investigators believe the occupant(s) of this vehicle may have critical information to share regarding this [the Idaho student murders] case."

Yet there was a problem with the BOLO. The Moscow authorities had disseminated the FBI's initial inaccurate determination of the Hyundai's year. In time, they would correct this error. But by then, the damage would have already been done.

FOUR LONG DAYS PASSED BEFORE the campus cops at Washington State University, the school not much more than a ten-minute or so drive across the state line from the Idaho murder house, got around to hunting for the car.

On November 29, at 12:38 a.m., not even a half hour into the start of his midnight–8:00 a.m. graveyard shift, Officer Daniel Tiengo decided to catch up on a stack of paperwork. It was a particularly slow time; the university was in the midst of its Thanksgiving break. And near the top of his pile was the bulletin the Moscow PD had circulated. It had been there for days.

Tiengo was hardworking, affable, a nighttime supervisor with a straggly, professorial goatee. Moments after he read the notice, he started tapping away at his computer, and a near match appeared on the screen. Bryan Kohberger, a grad student living in a university apartment compound on Northeast Valley Road, owned a 2015 white Hyundai Elantra.

Dutifully, Tiengo passed the baton to his late-night patrol sergeant, Curtis Whitman. Whitman was an old-guard campus cop, someone who had been deeply shaken by the decertification of a fellow officer for allegedly extorting sex from a coed in exchange for dropping an arrest for public intoxication. To defuse tensions on campus in the aftermath of that incident, he had appealed to students in a public forum, asking for their support and cooperation. And at the same difficult time, he also wanted them to grasp his sense of duty, his commitment to their safety. He was there to protect them, he pledged.

WHITMAN DIDN'T WASTE ANY TIME tracking the vehicle down. At 12:58 a.m.—precisely twenty minutes after Tiengo had initially identified a possible owner of the Suspect Vehicle 1—Whitman was staring through the nighttime darkness at a white Hyundai sitting in a graduate apartment complex parking lot. When he aimed his flashlight at the car, the numbers on the license plate were as distinct as those on top of an eye examination chart. He radioed his find back to his boss.

Tiengo now had a plate number to go with the car owner's name. And Tiengo quickly forwarded the intelligence to the Moscow PD.

But the team at headquarters showed no interest. The information from the WSU cop was catalogued, and then swiftly filed away. The BOLO had requested that the authorities search for a 2011–2013 white Hyundai Elantra. This one was a 2015 model.

MEANWHILE, ANOTHER CAR NOW SPARKED the team's interest. The team, in a sudden burst of inspiration, had landed on a new, intriguing idea—Kaylee Goncalves's recently purchased used silver gray Range Rover. Perhaps, they now wondered, the pretty blond woman had caught the malicious attention of one of the vehicle's previous owners. Over several intensive days, believing they were finally on to something, the detectives tried to locate all the names listed on the car's registration.

When they traveled up north to interview an individual with previous ties to the car, he at once turned belligerent; it didn't sit well with him that, by implication at least, he was being accused of four horrific murders. Tempers, according to one knowledgeable account, erupted. And, frustrated, without any other leads to gnaw at, the officers gave as good as they got. But in the end, like all the others tied to the Range Rover, it became clear he was innocent and they were forced to apologize. The investigators returned to Moscow in a deep funk, uncertain of their next move.

They had no idea they had already received the key necessary to unlock this case. And that it had been stored away in one of the team's computer files, forgotten and ignored.

TWENTY-TWO

———

In the end, the Hyundai was the only lead they had, and, desperate, they tried to leverage it. The premise, as Payne patiently explained it to the team assembled at the next early morning conference, was simple: sort through the mobile phone numbers that had pinged cell towers near the crime scene in the hours surrounding the murders. If one of the numbers belonged to someone whose name also appeared on their expanded master list of white Hyundai Elantra owners, then they had their suspect.

It was a very smart idea—unless the murderer was smarter. A shrewd killer might very well have turned off his phone before heading out to kill four people. And when they completed the search, the bottom line was a heartache: none of the owners of the suspiciously pinging cell phones also owned an even more suspicious white 2011–2016 Hyundai Elantra.

But investigations, like wars, proceed simultaneously on several fronts. And even as they were striking out, three hundred miles up north in the pleasant city of Meridian, the specialists at the Idaho State Police Forensic Services laboratory had been quietly laboring away. They had found a single trace source of male DNA on the button snap of the leather Ka-Bar sheath the killer had left tangled in the sheets on Maddie's bed. It was, they hoped, the solid clue that could crack the case wide open.

THE CONSUMER DNA KITS THAT are sold in any CVS need about 750 to 1,000 nanograms of the substance as a threshold amount to solve genetic mysteries. That's not much. It's smaller than a speck of floating dust and a whole lot less substantial. A single nanogram weighs a trillionth of a pound. There's nothing to it.

Crime scenes often contain a whole lot less DNA than that. Forensic teams will routinely wind up with only one hundred or so nanograms of DNA. Nevertheless, time after time, lab technicians have peered long and hard into their microscopes and wound up being able to apply even this minuscule amount to nail a criminal.

The Idaho lab's challenge, however, was that the DNA on the knife sheath was "touch" male DNA left by a finger that had brushed against the metal snap. And it amounted to less than one hundred nanograms. A whole lot less. In total, the scientists would grumble, about twenty cells. Maybe even fewer.

Getting the information they needed from a specimen that tiny was tough, but by November 20 they had processed a sufficient amount of DNA.

Now the mood in the lab took on a new energy. They just needed to jump through one more investigative hoop, and the case would be on its way to being solved. And this next exercise, they felt with a certainty reinforced by past experience, would be the easy part.

The Idaho lab swiftly ran the DNA profile they'd unearthed from the button snap of the knife sheath through CODIS. The FBI's Combined DNA Index System held an impressive inventory of genetic information, offering swift access to the entire body of DNA profiles collected from crime scenes throughout the country, as well as genetic samples from all convicted felons, sex offenders, and even unidentified human remains. There were over twenty million profiles in CODIS, and the Idaho team liked the odds of someone who had killed four people having acquired a criminal history.

Only the system couldn't make a match. The identity of the man whose DNA was on the button of the knife sheath was not in CODIS.

———

BUT THEN THEY GOT LUCKY.

To understand the genesis of what, improbably, happened next, it is necessary to go back eight years, to September 2014.

A sun-kissed Indian summer morning, then, as a kayaker paddled with impressive energy down the fast-moving waters of the Snake River. All of a sudden, his wandering gaze landed on an object floating limply in the distance beneath the Perrine Bridge in Jerome County, Idaho. Curious, he broke course to investigate—and discovered a woman's body.

Over the next four years, investigators headed down a winding and exhausting trail in an attempt to determine the identity of the woman, and why she'd wound up floating facedown in the cold waters of the Snake River. They combed the area, checking the local restaurants, motels, bus depots, and taxi services. Photos of what remained of the dead woman's face, as well as her fingerprints and DNA samples, were run through national databases. Fourteen states reached out to the Idaho State Police thinking the "Jane Doe" matched descriptions of missing persons they were pursuing. All the arduous detective work, however, led nowhere. In August 2020, the case was officially classified "inactive." The voluminous evidence folders stuffed into the dusty file drawers that were the burial grounds of the frigidly cold cases.

But then, in relatively rapid succession, a flurry of unforeseen, yet fortuitous, events occurred. For starters, Matthew Gamette, the director of the Idaho state forensics lab, was a scientist with a master's in microbiology. And he had been following with an avid attention the resourceful ways investigative genetic genealogy—IGG, in the parlance of the forensic trade—had lately been used to turn up the heat on cold cases. In 2018, to cite one celebrated example, California detectives had been at last able to identify the particularly vicious murderer and rapist known as the Golden State Killer by tying the DNA he had left at the crime scene to family members who had previously submitted their DNA voluntarily to public genetic databases. Gamette figured what had worked in California would work in Idaho, too. He applied for and won a $3 million grant from the federal Bureau of Justice Assistance to fund genetic testing for use in long-standing unsolved cases. Spurred by the grant of government dollars, Idaho officials announced that the state was seeking bids from private companies that had expertise in advanced forensic testing.

The bid was won by Othram, a small start-up company based outside of Houston, Texas. And one of the first seemingly dead-end cases Gamette sent their way was the mystery of the identity of the female corpse—the coroner had ruled suicide as the cause of death—that had been found seven years earlier drifting down the Snake River.

Othram solved the mystery. Their scientists were able to use the minuscule amount of DNA from the corpse that had been preserved over the years to assemble a clear genealogical history. And the many-branched genetic family tree that took root led police investigators to a name: that of a woman who had gone missing nearly a decade ago from her home in San Diego. Case closed.

Four months later, that unlikely success got Gamette thinking: What if Othram could use its unique capabilities not just on cold cases, but also on a very hot one? A case whose solution might very well be embedded in the microscopic DNA left on the button snap of a knife sheath.

TWENTY-THREE

———

Some scientists take pride in their lofty detachment. They prefer to work on big, eternal mysteries. But at Othram's gleaming, cutting-edge laboratory in a suburban high-tech corridor just north of Houston, Texas, there was a shared sense of a very practical quest. Two dozen or so assembled lab geeks had signed on for a do-gooder's crusade. And now they were brought into the Idaho murders case.

The company's mission had its idealistic roots in the shared vision of Othram's husband-and-wife founders. Drs. David and Kristen Mittelman's zealous plan was to use genetic science to free innocents who had been wrongly convicted and also help track down the actual criminals. There was, however, one immediate problem. To accomplish this on the scale the Mittelmans had grandly envisioned would be an expensive undertaking. Setting up a fully staffed lab and filling it with the sort of rarefied equipment, like a NovaSeq 6000, that can process DNA so it could be uploaded to a genetic database required a good deal of money.

Enter Charles Johnson. In the midst of a painful divorce, Johnson had fled from his marital home in San Francisco to the Texas suburb of the Woodlands, a burgeoning high-tech corridor just north of Houston. It was in this appealing suburb that Johnson, always gregarious, met the

Mittelmans. Over several intense conversations, Johnson grew intrigued with the unique genetic technology the company had developed to help solve cold cases. And when he met up with the Mittelmans again in San Francisco, at the end of a long dinner, he volunteered to do what he could to get them the money they needed.

Johnson, who had a Rolodex full of connections, soon introduced the two scientists to John Burbank. Burbank was a self-made billion-aire venture capitalist, the founder of Passport Capital, a thriving San Francisco–based hedge fund with $4 billion under management, and, no less significantly, someone with a deep thinker's appreciation for innovative ideas. And—more congenial symmetry—he was a reader who immediately recognized the company's name was a reference to the impenetrable black rock wall in Tolkien's *The Lord of the Rings.* In 2019, Burbank provided the crucial seed money Othram needed to get going in a significant way, writing a personal check for $2 million and raising another $2 million from, he'd offer with a financier's discretion, "sources."

It was a marriage made in start-up heaven—for a while. Burbank provided the checks and offered a veteran businessman's shrewd advice, and Johnson received a potentially lucrative chunk of stock for playing middleman to the Mittelmans. It was only later that the scientists dis-covered more about the man who had brokered the deal.

The banner headline above a hard-hitting article in the *Boston Globe* about Johnson was dismaying enough: "A race-baiting troll has found acceptance—in Trump's D.C." But the disclosures were more distress-ing: "He's argued that Black people are 'dumber' than white people, questioned whether six million Jews died in the Holocaust, was banned from Twitter for threatening a Black Lives Matter activist, and posed making a white power sign while standing next to white supremacist leader Richard Spencer." And now Johnson was a fairly significant stock-holder in their idealistic, justice-driven creation, a company where key scientists had relatives who had died in the Holocaust.

Johnson quickly offered apologies for his past beliefs. "I've evolved," he explained with terse contrition. He also suggested that many of his prior assertions had actually been role-playing. With a confiding yet somewhat puzzling intimacy, he let people know that he had been acting under orders from "intelligence agencies" and he was meticulously "constructing a cover identity."

The Mittelmans, however, remained chagrined. And this was the stormy situation blowing with disruptive fury through the labs at Othram as the request came from the Idaho authorities asking for assistance. To their credit, with the future of the investigation into the murdered students hanging in the balance, the Othram team put all that aside. Manning the NovaSeq 6000, they went to work.

Over several intense days, they did it. From a minute speck invisible to the naked eye, they had created a DNA profile that could now be uploaded to commercial genealogy services. From this tiny acorn, the scientists hoped, a family tree would take root and grow. And on one of its many branches they would find a killer.

The newly processed DNA profile was sent directly from the lab in Texas to the FBI's Quantico facility. It arrived at the same hulking sandstone building where the bureau's analysts had struggled to identify the car spotted outside the murder house. And another failure, the tech team realized, would be devastating.

FBI FORENSIC GENEALOGISTS LIKE TO say that their particular profession had its roots in the Book of Genesis, where the litany of "begats" laid out humankind's original family tree. Now, however, centimorgans pointed the way. This was the unit of measurement—the name a turn-of-the-century tribute to Thomas Hunt Morgan, a pioneering biologist—that quantified the genetic ties that bind people together. The higher the amount of shared centimorgans, the greater the probability of a common ancestor. Score a shared sixty or more on the centimorgan scale with someone, and no doubt about it, you were related.

The FBI probers found the initial foundational information they needed to launch their search for shared centimorgans on readily accessible websites like GEDmatch and FamilyTreeDNA (other popular sites, for example, Ancestry.com and 23andMe, were more reluctant to make the information people had given them available to law enforcement). This allowed them to build up "clusters," as they were known, of families and each group of relatives became another strong limb on the family tree that was taking shape.

But lab work would only take the investigators so far. To give flesh-and-blood context to what they were finding, they had to roll up their sleeves and do things the old-fashioned way (that is, relatively "old-fashioned"; the Internet was a vast repository of helpful information and documents) and chase down birth announcements, obituaries, and court records.

At this stage, they were just gathering information, not trying to force or shape the findings with any preconceived notions. The operating rule was that the family clusters would all need to be definitively filled out, and until this laborious exercise was completed, it would be precipitous to jump to any conclusion. Therefore, there was no sense of an impending game-changing moment when the interconnected centimorgans led the way to the marriage of Henrietta Kathrine Votino to Michael Francis Kohberger Sr. on June 17, 1954, in New York City. And even as the limbs of this family tree spread eventually through the generations to the birth of Bryan Christopher Kohberger on November 21, 1994, in Pennsylvania, there was no intimation that the puzzle was about to clarify.

However, soon the incriminating coincidences began mounting up. The DNA on the knife sheath button had ultimately led them to a grad student who was enrolled at Washington State University—which was about ten miles away from the house on King Road. And, they discovered, he could make the trip in the white 2015 Hyundai Elantra that was registered in his name. The FBI investigators now knew, as any good cop would know, that there was no need to look any further. They had found their suspect.

WHAT HAPPENED NEXT, THOUGH, REMAINS filed away in the still-secret history of this case. For while the FBI, as early as December 11, 2022, had identified Bryan Kohberger as a person of interest in the four student murders, they did not share the discovery at this point with either the Moscow Police or the Idaho state troopers. Rather, the decision was made, people with knowledge of the deliberations would confide in low voices, to keep the name to themselves.

Why? One theory had it that the bureau was simply being cautious. An IGG determination was not the sort of evidence that could lead to an indictment. It could never, according to Justice Department practice, even be cited in an arrest warrant. Its use in solving cold cases was one thing, but this attempt to use genetic genealogy to target a suspect in an active investigation was an entirely different matter. And a disturbing one. The best IGG could offer was a hypothesis, and a dubious one at that. It presented a conclusion forged out of a newfangled scientific technique that had yet to be fully tested in a court of law. Sure, IGG could maybe help point the way. But before an arrest could be made, the detectives would still need to do the legwork to build a case that would stand up under heavy scrutiny in a courtroom. So why muddy the investigative waters? Perhaps the bureau felt it would be better for the taskforce to go about its job methodically. Let them build their case from the bottom up rather than start with a suspect. That way there'd be no fears that the process could later be impugned by a sly defense attorney. No one could charge that the authorities had it in for the suspect and had tailored things to incriminate him.

Or there was another theory and this one was a lot less flattering. As these observers saw it, the FBI's decision was predicated entirely on self-interest. This was the bureau's triumph, and they were unwilling to share the glory. Here was a chance to polish a politically tarnished reputation with one very public arrest. And they didn't want to be robbed of this prize.

But whatever the reason, as the Kohbergers packed up the white Hyundai to head east for the holidays on December 12, the FBI had decided to begin covertly watching the father and son's every move once they left Washington. And neither Bryan nor Michael Kohberger ever suspected a thing.

And for that matter, neither did the Moscow taskforce.

TWENTY-FOUR

The bureau's watchers called it a "hatbox operation," and the jargon was a bit of an anachronism. It was a throwback to an era when G-men sporting fedoras over their Brylcreemed hair would be out in force on the street to monitor a target's every move. Back then, a sea of hats would box the suspect in. These days, the watchers have a few more tricks at their disposal—undercover vehicles, surveillance vans, low-flying fixed-wing planes, and that's just for starters—but the name has stuck. And on the morning of December 12, 2022, when the white Hyundai Elantra, Bryan Kohberger at the wheel, his father, Michael, riding shotgun in the front seat, pulled out of its space in the parking lot fronting 1630 NE Valley Road in Pullman, Washington, the surveillance plan was hatbox all the way.

The commitment to stealth was no less meticulous. For not only were the agents determined to keep their activity secret from the chief suspect in a quadruple homicide, but, for reasons shaped by a private logic, they were also set on making sure the Moscow taskforce had no inkling, either. As the watchers went to work, they kept their eyes on the prize but also watched their backs.

The local team never knew their federal partners in the case had a match on the knife sheath DNA. Or that the bureau was now intent on tracking the suspect's every move.

But by the day's end, the hatbox operation had turned into a colossal screwup. In their determination not to tip their hand to the Moscow taskforce, the watchers had decided not to pick up the Kohbergers until the car got well out of the area. This didn't seem a problem; they knew what route the travelers would be taking. But the bureau's supposition had been wrong. And the white Hyundai, along with its invaluable passengers, had seemingly vanished.

THERE'S NOT MUCH TO LOMA, Colorado—barely 1,300 residents were scattered about on a few big farmsteads. But US Route 6 passed straight through the center of town, and in 2015 the Colorado Department of Transportation thought it was high time to install Loma's first traffic light. It went up at the bustling (things being relative, of course) intersection of Route 6 and Highway 139. It wasn't long after that when the town's engineers decided that as long as they were going to all this trouble, they might as well affix an automated license plate reader to the light pole, too.

And so on December 13, when the surveillance team was frantically scrolling through the thousands of images in several states caught on automated license plate readers (ALPRs, as the instruments were universally known), the one in Loma came up a winner. It caught Washington State plate CFB-8708. The white 2015 Hyundai Elantra registered to Bryan Kohberger.

With this sighting, the hatbox op was once again underway. This was their second chance, and they were determined not to fumble it.

Yet it wasn't long after the vigilant watchers on the ground and in the air had resumed their monitoring that they were once again in danger of losing their suspect. Lights flashing, an Indiana sheriff had ordered the Kohbergers to the side of the road.

The team was stunned. The encounter had several predictable outcomes, and nearly all were dangerous. Had a conscientious Indiana sheriff connected the white Hyundai to the BOLO issued by Moscow

PD? Was he about to make an arrest before the final incriminating pieces had been fitted into the puzzle? If that happened, it had the potential to be a catastrophe. The suspect would be alerted, and in the aftermath, if he followed the advice of a canny defense attorney, the army of investigators would never have the opportunity to make their airtight case. And—another rub—the bureau would be deprived of its moment of glory.

There were tactical concerns, too. Was the suspect armed? Would someone who they believed had killed four people hesitate to kill again? Was the sheriff's deputy in danger of becoming another victim? Perhaps they should abandon their cover and intervene before the situation escalated. Didn't the possible threat to a lawman's life supersede everything else? Or, another troubling consideration: maybe Kohberger wouldn't stay put on the shoulder. He could gun the Hyundai and race down the highway. A decision had to be made.

Finally, the order went out from command to stand back—at least for now. And so they watched, antsy yet disciplined, as the traffic stop began to play out. At the first sign that things were falling apart, they were prepared to hit the sirens and the flashing lights and swoop in. But to their immense relief, it wasn't long before the white car had pulled back onto the interstate and was once again heading east.

What was that all about? the watchers asked one another. But within just minutes, an Indiana state trooper, lights flashing, had directed the white car to pull over again. What indeed was going on?

FOR DAYS, MICHAEL KOHBERGER HAD been struggling, however obliquely, to get a handle on the overwhelming sense of dread that had been weighing on him in the aftermath of his meeting up with his son at the Pullman-Moscow airport. He had not tried to think about its origins, Michael later told relatives. But now Michael began to suspect that there must be something purposeful guiding the rapid succession of police stops. Each was one part of a whole, and its meaning was about to be made clear. Michael braced himself for what would happen next.

"Please get your license and registration," the trooper barked. He stood outside the passenger-side window and spoke across Michael as if he weren't there. Bryan once again hunted for the documents.

"When you were driving by me there," the trooper continued, his voice now easier, "you were a little too close to the back of the semi. You had only one car length."

Bryan, respectful, cooperative, replied that only a few miles down the highway they had been stopped for an identical infraction.

The trooper seemed suddenly suspicious. This was his stretch of highway; there wouldn't be another statie patrolling close by. Why lie?

Michael jumped in to clear up the confusion. He explained that it had been a sheriff's deputy.

That made sense, the trooper decided. "It was a county guy. It was like a black SUV?"

Then Michael decided to speak up. He once again launched into a convoluted account of the fatal SWAT team shoot-out at the off-campus apartment house earlier that morning in Pullman.

And once again, his telling left the lawman perplexed. If it was a piece in a larger puzzle, the trooper clearly had no grasp of the problem that needed to be solved. "Where were y'all heading to?" he asked, eager to return to firmer ground.

In unison, the Kohbergers replied: "Pennsylvania."

"PA? That's a long haul. You guys scared of planes?"

Everyone shared a good-natured laugh. After only a warning, and again no ticket, the trooper wished them a safe trip.

As the car pulled back onto the highway, Michael played back the encounter in his mind. His son's emotional temperature, he recalled, hadn't appeared to have jumped a notch. Only later, he'd wonder to a relative, whether that was the demeanor of someone who had nothing to hide. Or was it the icy calm of someone incapable of feeling fear?

———

THE FBI WATCHERS, TOO, HAD their unanswered questions. Were the Indiana patrol officers on to something? Had they made the Hyundai? Or, equally implausible, was it simply what it seemed to be: two consecutive stops for tailgating?

As for Michael, now that they were edging closer to the familiar dense forests and humpbacked peaks of the Poconos, he found himself wishing that this journey would go on forever. That they would just drive and drive. For he had begun at last to put a name on what he suspected he would find at the end of the trail.

TWENTY-FIVE

The FBI watchers were thankful for the snow. It had started to come down in a swirl of thick, white flakes over the winding Albrightsville, Pennsylvania, roads, and that meant Bryan Kohberger would very likely be staying put.

Earlier that afternoon, December 16, at just about 2:30, the Hyundai carrying the Kohbergers had completed its cross-country journey. The family lived in a fraying white clapboard house in a gated community called Indian Mountain Lakes Village, although the name was a bit of a mystery since there was neither an Indian, a mountain, nor a lake in sight. A decade ago, the residences had largely been modest summer cottages for families wanting to escape from the heat and tumult of New York and Philadelphia. But now full-time residents were the norm. Still, a throwback to the community's grander days, there were a manned sentry box and a pair of white boom gates at the main entrance. The high security was meant to keep the homeowners safe and sound from all the many dangers that lurked outside. However, after the FBI team saw the boom gates raise high and Bryan Kohberger drive through, one of the observers couldn't suppress an ironic speculation: they very possibly had just let a quadruple murderer into their midst.

The falling snow also gave the bureau another advantage—the time to think.

From the start, they had been flirting with disaster. First, losing track of the targeted vehicle would've been bad enough. Then, not one, but two unexpected highway traffic stops, and each a disaster just waiting to happen. By now the bureau had learned that the Indiana authorities' vigilance had been prompted by a drug interdiction operation that zeroed in on out-of-state license plates. But if Kohberger had behaved differently, if an Indiana cop had the nationwide BOLO about a white Hyundai Elantra taped to his dashboard, it was anyone's guess what would have happened. And so they considered: if this op was indeed accident-prone, then maybe it would be good practical politics to be able to share the blame, even if it also meant sharing the glory. Besides, they had not originally anticipated that there would be a Pennsylvania component to the hunt. The locals would need to get involved; the jurisdictional issues were impossible to ignore. But, most persuasive, they had come to realize it just didn't make sense to keep the Moscow taskforce out of the loop. It had grown clearer and clearer that they would need their help to bring this case to the nearly ironclad juncture where an arrest would be legally possible.

The snow kept falling, and they kept thinking. Until at last the bureau team, like good soldiers, finally did what it should have done days earlier.

ALL ALONG, CORPORAL BRETT PAYNE had been praying for a name, and now he had it. On December 19, the bureau, according to the official records, shared what had been discovered after the forensic genealogists had extended the DNA-rooted family tree to its farthest branch. Unofficial insider accounts, however, peg the notification to a day, maybe even two, earlier (although those might be attempts by the FBI to mitigate the sting of their self-interested delay). But while there is debate over the actual date, there is no disagreement that once Payne had Bryan Kohberger's name he jumped into action.

Early on, he entered the name and the license plate number the feds had shared into the Motor Vehicle Records system. The computer screen promptly displayed a state driver's license. It listed Bryan Kohberger as a white male, a sturdy 6' and 185 pounds. Which, Payne told himself, was pretty close to the broad description of the intruder Dylan Mortensen had seen. As well as, he also matter-of-factly conceded, a few thousand other guys on either the U of I or WSU campuses.

Then he turned to the photograph. Was this the face of a killer? He stared at it intently, but for all his scrutiny, he saw nothing out of the ordinary. Nevertheless, he kept boring in on the photo, and just like that, something caught his gaze: the eyebrows. They were bushy. Same as those of the intruder Dylan had spotted. And this small confirming detail, while too subjective to be admissible in a courtroom, further nudged his sense of urgency.

Armed with a name, he could also hunt for a cell phone number. Here, for once, he got lucky. For when he searched the department's own records, to his immense satisfaction he learned that back in August, Kohberger had been stopped for a routine traffic infraction. A Latah County sheriff's deputy had nailed the grad student for driving without a seat belt and, as was the standard practice, had included Kohberger's phone number in the summons report.

With that number in hand, he reached for another file. In the inchoate days of the hunt, he had blindly bombarded the phone companies with search warrants requesting information about any devices that had pinged the cell towers in the vicinity of the King Road house between 3:00 and 5:00 a.m. on the morning the murders occurred. Now he could return to this previously unsatisfying list in a more purposeful way. He searched to see if Kohberger's number had been recorded; this discovery would be the smoking—or more accurately, the pinging—gun.

Payne found nothing. Kohberger's phone had not been caught at the crucial time by a cell tower in the vicinity of the murder house. It was not encouraging, but he decided to store this knowledge away until, he hoped, another part of the puzzle might give it a more meaningful context.

And so, undeterred, on December 23—more than five weeks after the murders—he decided to investigate what Kohberger's phone had been up to around the time of the homicides. He sent a search warrant to AT&T, the provider of Kohberger's cell service, requesting the records for the number between November 12, 2022, at 12:00 a.m. and November 14 at 12:00 a.m.

A detailed report arrived back at his desk that same day. And with that began the steady, careful paperchase. Working side by side with Benjamin Dean, an experienced FBI special agent on the Salt Lake City field office's Cellular Analysis Survey Team, they set out to chart the interaction between Kohberger's pinging phone and the time-coded surveillance videos that had captured passing glimpses of the white Hyundai Elantra in the fateful hours after midnight on November 13. When they were done, they had put together a grimly compelling narrative.

According to their reconstruction, Kohberger—or at least his phone—had left his apartment in Pullman at 2:47 a.m. on November 13 and had been heading south when abruptly it stopped reporting to the network. Turned off? Switched to airplane mode? Or, for that matter, the phone could have traveled into a rural area with no cell reception; this was northern Idaho, after all.

But those possibilities seemed highly unlikely when the videos that had captured what appeared to be Kohberger's car filled in the picture. There was the white Hyundai—the infamous Suspect Vehicle 1— recorded making three slow, laborious passes by 1122 King Road from 3:29 a.m. to nearly 4:00 a.m. Then the car returned a fourth time at 4:04 a.m., only to abruptly disappear from sight. Yet at 4:20, there it was again, hightailing it out of Moscow at a breakneck speed.

And just as suddenly—at a telltale 4:48 a.m.—the cell phone pinged back to life. Heading out south from Moscow on US 95, the device continued to ping its way on a circuitous route through the countryside. But at nearly 5:30 a.m., the phone was making its way back to Pullman—just at the same time as surveillance cameras spotted the white Hyundai crawling back to the WSU campus neighborhood.

There was also a tantalizing coda to the drama Payne and the FBI expert had stitched together: At 9:00 that Sunday morning, Kohberger's phone left Pullman and headed back toward Moscow. Then for nine long minutes—an interlude heavy with mystery—the phone was pinging like crazy off the cell tower that serviced the King Road house. For many of the cops on the taskforce, the explanation was clear: the murderer was returning to the scene of the crime.

But not so fast, Fry had challenged his team leader. What about the gap when Kohberger's phone went silent? It included the precise time when the murders had occurred. How could the team tie Kohberger to the crimes if they couldn't even prove he had been in the house when the murders happened?

Payne, always resourceful, had an answer—or at least a theory—handy. It had its antecedents in Arthur Conan Doyle's "The Adventure of Silver Blaze," where Holmes's canny solution had been prompted by the "curious incident" of the dog that didn't bark. Payne, too, had found reassurance in a "negative fact."

"Individuals," he would write, "can either leave their cellular telephone at a different location before committing a crime or turn their cellular telephone off prior going to a location to commit a crime. This is done by subjects in an effort to avoid alerting law enforcement that a cellular device associated with them was in a peculiar area where a crime is committed." And, although he didn't come out and say it, a further implication was clear: this shrewdness was precisely the sort of precaution a graduate student in criminal justice setting out to commit the perfect crime would employ.

Payne was now convinced: the cell phone records and the Suspect 1 car videos inexorably pointed toward Bryan Kohberger.

But he also understood that no judge would sign an arrest warrant for murder that was stitched together with all this speculation. And, he further conceded when pressed by Chief Fry, all the pinging phones might, under close scrutiny, add up to nothing than a lot of noise. The discomforting truth was that cell phone towers cast a wide net, often as far as twelve to fourteen miles. In a town like Moscow, that would take in a lot of territory. However tempting it was to claim the data was irrefutable evidence, the reality was that being in the vicinity was not the same thing at all as being at an exact address.

And so as Christmas came and went, the hunters gathered once more on December 26 in the PD's conference room. Only now the discussion turned to refuse—garbage cans, actually—and just like that, things started to improve.

AS IT HAPPENED, IN ALBRIGHTSVILLE there was talk in the Kohberger household about garbage, too. Melissa, the older of Bryan's two sisters, had come home for the holidays from New Jersey. For over a decade, she had been a practicing psychologist who specialized in helping families deal with thorny issues. And now without really trying, she began to notice certain things about her own family. There was Bryan wearing white surgical gloves as he suctioned the Hyundai's upholstery and trunk with a shop vacuum. Then there he was in the kitchen late at night sorting his day's personal detritus into plastic Ziploc bags. And though she had not set out to spy, and afterward wished she never had seen it at all, there was her brother sneaking out after midnight. Like a man on a mission, he walked down the long drive in the starlit chill to deposit the family's trash bags in a next-door neighbor's bins. When she put a name and purpose to all she'd been witnessing, it left her shaking.

At last, though, Melissa found the will to share her increasingly certain deduction with her father. Michael listened, yet he could not respond. A long, agonized silence filled the room, until at last he turned his back and walked away.

TWENTY-SIX

To hear the members of the Moscow taskforce tell it, the entire investigation could be divided into Before the Match and After the Match, and the Match was Kohberger's DNA. But for the Pennsylvania state troopers who only got involved at the tail end, when they were called on to bring the case across the finish line, the case's penultimate moment would forever after be known as the Great Trash Robbery.

Major Chris Paris of the Pennsylvania State Police had been hand-picked by the FBI to command the operation, and he was a shrewd choice. He looked like a linebacker, and he did have a gruff, no-nonsense edge. But he was also a thoughtful, scholarly man; he'd graduated magna cum laude from the University of Scranton, and he'd gone on to get a law degree from Temple. Even more valuable given the circumstances, Paris possessed a lawyerly sense of discretion.

Quietly convening a sparse, eight-person working group, he shared the secret that the FBI had a suspect in the Idaho quadruple homicide case in the crosshairs and the target was right on their home turf, in Albrightsville. He let that sink in, and then he issued a steely warning: a leak and the whole case might be blown. And if that happened, he threatened gravely, well, that would be the end of the leaker's career.

With the warning out of the way, he outlined the mission. A select team of troopers would keep a covert eye on the suspect, and then when the time was right, they'd sneak in and steal Kohberger's garbage.

The operational unit was recruited from Troop N, the state police barracks down the road from Albrightsville, and they were all experienced officers—"the best of the best," Paris would brag. For four days and nights, keeping their distance and hiding in the winter shadows, they had their eyes glued on Kohberger. As things played out, their professional assessment pretty much mirrored Melissa Kohberger's amateur finding: the graduate student was up to something. For now, though, they watched, and they waited.

Then on December 27, the pace accelerated. Paris convened his team and announced that the bureau had flashed the green light. Next he pointed to Trooper Brian Noll of the Criminal Investigations Division. "I'm counting on you," he announced.

In one of the investigation's small coincidences, it turned out that Noll had previously worked with the tiny Texas lab whose inventive scientific handiwork had set this raid in motion. Othram had intervened to restore his shattered lawman's faith.

COPS WILL TELL YOU THAT some cases stay with you. You can't let them go. They ride shotgun on your thoughts. For Brian Noll, it was the case of "Beth Doe." It was a grisly murder mystery that had frustrated the authorities for over forty years.

Just days before Christmas in 1976, three suitcases had been tossed off a bridge that spanned the Lehigh River in White Haven, Pennsylvania. They missed the water, and landed on the grassy shoulder running along nearby rural Interstate 80. When the cops opened them, each of the three valises contained pieces of a dismembered female body. The victim, an autopsy showed, had been sexually assaulted, strangled, and then shot in the neck. She had been carrying a nine-month-old female fetus.

Twenty or so years later, Trooper Noll was assigned the task of seeing if there were any new leads. Noll stuck with it for years, never giving up, but he got nowhere. His failure ground away at him, a stinging personal defeat.

Then in November 2020, forty-four years after the body parts had been found, DNA extracted from Beth Doe's skeletal remains was sent to the Othram lab in Texas. Despite all the decades, the butchered woman was identified. On the heels of this breakthrough, an alleged killer was arrested. And the murder case that had been front and center in Noll's thoughts for so long had been solved.

AND NOW NOLL WAS BACK on the hunt. It was nearly 4:00 a.m., and he crept with a furtive concentration. He listened to the night noises, waiting, taking his time. He knew stealth was crucial. If his presence was detected, if Kohberger had an inkling that he was being watched, then he might run, and, at this inconclusive point in the investigation, there was little that could be done to stop him.

And yet the absurdity of the situation also registered. Noll reached into the garbage can and grabbed two plastic bags, and held them high in the air like trophies. He wanted the troopers huddled in the adjacent woods to see. But then he had a sudden, sickening thought: *I should have brought replacements.* What if Kohberger came out to deposit another bag? He'd wonder how the others had suddenly vanished. But there was nothing he could do now, so he simply clutched his pilfered treasures filled with detritus close to his chest and made his way through the darkness and back to a waiting SUV.

Events from there proceeded with an almost mechanical precision. A parcel filled with the purloined garbage was shipped priority across the country to Meridian, Idaho. There, in the state police forensic lab, the technicians lifted several DNA samples from the debris.

Only to fail. They could not find any DNA profile that precisely matched the DNA they had previously recovered from the button of the knife sheath. Which left two possibilities. Either Bryan Kohberger, the methodical criminal justice student, had made sure that any material that might contain his DNA did not go into his family's trash, or they had the wrong man.

They were shaken, but they had come too far to give up. And when they repeated their comparative analysis, a startling discovery was made. The DNA profile obtained from the trash belonged with a conclusive 99.9998 percent certainty to the father of the man whose DNA was on the knife sheath.

Michael Kohberger, despite all of his guarded silence, had branded his son a killer.

THE NEXT DAY, DECEMBER 29, Brett Payne sat down at his desk on the second floor of the Moscow police headquarters to finalize the arrest warrant. Oddly, there was no sense of triumph. Like any hunter, he knew that having the prey in his sights was not sufficient. Dozens of things could still go wrong.

Payne felt that every moment counted. Rather than emailing the warrant, where, he worried without any real justification, it might get ignored by a clerk, he hand-delivered the nineteen-page document to the courthouse.

Moments after Judge Megan Marshall signed off, a call was made to Pennsylvania.

"It's a go!" Major Paris was told.

TWENTY-SEVEN

———

"Dynamic entry" was only used to serve an arrest warrant when the threat matrix was Code Red. The team charged in loud and strong, pounding down doors, breaking windows, and setting off explosive devices. The strategy was not just to surprise the suspect, but to scare the living daylights out of him. Because there's one thing that's always rising up in the mind of any tactical cop crashing through the front door: if the target's waiting inside ready to shoot, tactics wouldn't count for much. This was his turf. He had the advantage. And if he was determined to put up a fight, bad things could happen.

At just after midnight on December 30, a Pennsylvania State Police Emergency Response Team (SERT) assembled at the gray, barnlike Troop N barracks in Hazleton. There were about twenty-four of them: the usual sixteen entry team members and maybe eight sharpshooters. And they were packing heavy. Glock .40-caliber pistols were generally the weapon of choice, and the point men as a rule carried two pistols. The officers who'd be the first through the door were also armed with stubby black HK MP5 submachine guns; it was a brutal weapon, particularly in an enclosed space. The backups had short-barreled Remington 870 12-gauges; it was a shotgun meant for killing, not wounding. Over military-style camo uniforms, the team wore heavy, load-bearing tactical body armor fitted out with Level IV strike plates. The early morning arrest of Bryan Kohberger would be a Code Red op, dynamic entry all the way. When you were heading off to arrest someone accused of butchering four people in cold blood, you didn't take chances.

THE SERT TEAM PILED INTO a couple of specially outfitted Ford E-350 extended-body vans for the half-hour ride to Albrightsville. A contingent of Troop N staties followed as backup. All in all, there were about forty officers. It might as well have been an invading army.

But as the force approached the rural community dotted with playgrounds and volleyball courts where the Kohbergers lived, the lead van came to a sudden halt. The entrance to Indian Mountain Lakes was blocked by a pair of white boom gates; in the early hour of the morning, before the guard reported to work, a code had to be entered into a sentry box for the poles to rise. And none of the heavily armed officers had the code.

A few of the tough-guy SERT team members, according to the bemused story that buzzed around Troop N in the aftermath, wanted to just plow through. But cooler heads prevailed. As the force waited impatiently in the vans, a state trooper tracked down an acquaintance in the community, and the entry code was obtained. With the gate at last raised high, the force proceeded. It was 1:30 in the morning, and they followed in a tight formation down a curling road until they reached Lamsden Drive.

IT WAS SO QUIET IT seemed as if the cocking of a single rifle would rouse people from their slumber. The team, however, exited the vans and took their positions without being noticed. Then all hell broke loose. Windows shattered. Explosive charges boomed. The SERT team stormed the white clapboard house.

There was no need to fire a shot.

They found Bryan Kohberger in the kitchen. Despite the hour, he was awake. He was wearing shorts, a T-shirt, and latex gloves. He had been scrupulously stuffing his personal trash into Ziploc plastic baggies, still convinced he was smarter than anyone else.

Someone grabbed him by the collar and heaved Kohberger up from his chair. He seemed stunned as the handcuffs were snapped onto his wrists. The team commander insisted that a protective cordon be assembled around the suspect. Just a precaution, he explained.

Trembling, handcuffed, surrounded by towering troopers, Bryan Kohberger was led down the driveway to the waiting van.

TWENTY-EIGHT

———

Bryan Kohberger was talking. In the first hours after his arrest, the suspect was not only willing to discuss the case but seemed quite pleased to do so. Of course, Kohberger said, he knew about the four murders in Idaho; everyone in the area did. After all, he offered with a disarming openness, he lived only about ten miles from the murder house. He kept on talking, genial and cooperative, denying any involvement in the events, for nearly a quarter of an hour. But as the interrogators' questions grew more pointed, Kohberger grew terse. Finally, he said, "Enough." He wanted a lawyer, only he couldn't afford to pay for one.

At about 9:30 on the morning of December 30, a call went out to the office of Jason LaBar, the county's chief public defender. In his decades of practice, LaBar had appeared before the courts in more than twenty capital cases. He was also a local guy; his family's deep roots in the area reached far back to colonial times. And in his days at nearby Bangor Area High School, he had been a three-letter man, and thirty years later, had been recently elected to the school's Athletic Hall of Fame. He still looked like the rock-solid, broad-shouldered, crew-cutted halfback you'd want to hand the ball when the game was on the line. He could handle the pressures that'd come with this sort of case, the authorities decided.

Still, when LaBar's secretary called to let him know that he would be representing the man accused of killing the four Idaho students, he hung up without a word. He was in his daughter's orthodontist's office in New Jersey, and he was in no mood for any jokes; the thought of what the teenager's braces were costing had soured his disposition.

After all their years together, though, his secretary knew her boss well enough not to be intimidated. When she called back to insist that she had not been playing around, LaBar felt, he'd say, "as stunned as if a door had slammed in my face." Like everyone else, he'd been following the events in Idaho, but he never could've imagined the trail would lead across the country to his own backyard. When his daughter's appointment was over, he told her he wouldn't be able to take her to the mall to check out the post-Christmas sales. The most famous case in the country, he explained, "has fallen into my lap."

Friday had been a half day at the public defenders' office, and when he arrived he had the place to himself. He was thankful for the quiet because he needed to concentrate. He'd be representing Kohberger in the hearing for his extradition to Idaho, and it was necessary to get a working knowledge of the state's statutes. If his client wanted to fight being sent back across the country to stand trial, LaBar wanted to have a viable battle plan. He pored over the Idaho canons, and then hurried to the office's law library to research cases where writs of habeas corpus had been filed to protect the accused from being transported to other jurisdictions. He was feverishly taking notes on a yellow pad, when another realization intruded. Every New Year's Eve, he'd meet with a bunch of his old high school football teammates and their wives. They'd sit around in front of a blazing fire talking about the outcomes of games they'd competed in a lifetime ago, play Monopoly, and drink Jägermeister shots while they waited for the Times Square ball to drop. He called his wife and asked her to let the other couples know that they wouldn't be making it this year; he had work to do. Then he returned to the case books and waited for it to get dark.

He knew that once the word got out that he was representing Kohberger, the press would be monitoring his every move. His plan was to sneak off to the jail.

THE MONROE COUNTY JAIL WAS just a short drive from Main Street, but still it was out in the country and away from any homes. The roads were unlit, and for the entire journey LaBar kept checking his rearview mirror to see if any headlights were on his tail. It remained pitch-black the entire way. His strategy had worked; he had not been followed.

The prison grounds were surrounded by a high chain-link fence that had curls of razor wire at the top. LaBar, who knew his way around the jail, parked on the far side of the compound across from the chain-link door that served as the visitors' entrance. The guard let him in without challenge; he had been expected.

Feeling the cold, he walked down a gravel path harshly illuminated by an overhead spotlight for a couple of minutes to a steel-plated door. He buzzed, and the door immediately opened; here, too, it was as if the guard had been waiting for his arrival.

Moments later, a little after 5:00 p.m., LaBar was seated in a windowless interrogation room. The room was as brightly lit as an operating theater. Bryan Kohberger was led in and took a seat directly opposite him.

LaBar silently took a quick measure of the accused killer, and his first reaction was surprise. He was not sure what he had expected, but he was nevertheless unprepared for what he saw: Kohberger looked, he'd say, "normal." He had the sort of open, intelligent face and unblinking eyes that might have easily belonged to one of the young assistant district attorneys that LaBar went up against on an almost daily basis in the courtroom. For someone who had been charged with four murders, Kohberger seemed remarkably calm. LaBar felt none of the trepidation, the defensiveness, or, for that matter, the anger that usually enveloped his clients when he sat across from them in the county jail. Kohberger's gaze continued to hold steady on him, and to the lawyer's reading, it felt disapproving, as if this were all a mistake that would soon be rectified.

LaBar began with a warning. He made it clear to Kohberger that he would be representing him only in the extradition hearing. Therefore, he did not want to hear any specific details about the case.

With that out of the way, the lawyer asked if his new client wanted to release a statement to the press. The arrest was national news, and his guilt was being treated as a foregone conclusion. Kohberger, he suggested, might feel it was necessary to respond.

Kohberger agreed without hesitation, his voice firm. He wanted people to know that he "was eager to be exonerated." And he wanted his lawyer to understand that "this is not who I am."

LaBar listened with a studious attention. He was struck, he'd say, by how "calm" and "intelligent" Kohberger appeared. Murder, the lawyer instinctively felt, seemed "a little out of character" for the man to whom he was talking.

Kohberger had the last word. As LaBar was packing his yellow pad back into his briefcase, preparing to leave, Kohberger said it was important that he make one thing clear. He had not killed anyone. All he knew about the crime, about any of the victims, was what he had read in the newspapers.

IN PULLMAN, WASHINGTON, MEANWHILE, AT 7:15 on the morning after Kohberger's arrest, a team of police officers stood on the landing outside the suspect's apartment.

An officer's fist hammered on the door. "Police department! Search warrant! Come to the door!"

There was no response, and so he turned a key in the lock. He opened the door, but did not enter. Standing on the threshold with his service Glock drawn and extended as if ready to fire, he barked, "Show yourself."

No one came forward, but this was no surprise. The officers knew the tenant was in a jail cell on the other side of the country. Still, they had no solid notion at this point of whether Kohberger had any accomplices. It was better to be safe than sorry.

The forensic team put on protective gloves and booties and swarmed in.

In the bedroom, the officers found a computer tower and an Amazon Fire TV Stick, and they carted them off for further examination. At the same time, the forensic team proceeded with a disciplined attention, searching the little apartment for bloodstains, skin cells, and animal hair that had come from the house on King Road.

But the officers did not find a knife, or dark-colored clothing, or a mask. There wasn't even a shower curtain that could be examined for any trace evidence that might have been splattered when a killer had been frantically attempting to wash away any clues. The trash can was empty, too. Nothing was discovered that immediately confirmed the right man had been arrested.

At 1:00 p.m. that same day, in the wood-paneled city council chambers in the Moscow City Hall on Third Street, Chief Fry held a hastily arranged press conference.

For six weeks, he had endured sharp criticism as the investigation had dragged on without resolution; the constant reminder that the murders had occurred in his town and on his watch; the solemn promises he had made to the victims' parents, which he had begun to wonder if he could fulfill—and now he had accomplished all he had set out to do. He stood at the podium, and took a deep breath before he began, trying to rein in his emotions. "Last night," he said, and his voice immediately wavered. He paused, then: "In conjunction with the Pennsylvania State Police and the Federal Bureau of Investigation, detectives arrested twenty-eight-year-old Bryan Christopher Kohberger in Albrightsville, Pennsylvania . . ."

The words trailed off. His eyes welled with tears, and he blinked them away. Then he found the resolve to continue.

". . . on a warrant for the murders of Ethan, Xana, Madison, and Kaylee."

THAT NIGHT IN ALBRIGHTSVILLE, THE Kohbergers received a call that took them by surprise. It was from one of their son's former professors, Dr. Katherine Ramsland. The name struck a chord. Maryann Kohberger had heard her son talking with respect and enthusiasm about the DeSales University professor, a celebrated authority on serial killers. After the arrest, a lot of people had been telephoning, especially the press, and she had scrupulously refused to talk. It was all too painful. But she wanted to hear what Dr. Ramsland had to say.

Later, the professor would adamantly refuse to comment on any aspect of the case, including any discussions she may or may not have had with the Kohbergers. But according to the version of the conversation the Kohbergers had confided to a friend, Dr. Ramsland offered her help. She felt unable to make, the professor reportedly began, any judgment about Bryan's guilt or innocence. However, if the family needed any advice as the case proceeded, she would be glad to share her expertise. Bryan, she went on, had been one of her most promising students.

The Kohbergers were seduced. This was the single small kindness that had come their way since all the wretchedness had begun. And the timing was propitious. From the moment the SWAT team had charged into their home in the still of the night, guns leveled, smashing glass and pounding through doors, their lives had turned into something that did not seem possible. The sense of disconnection to any previous reality had been overpowering. At this low moment, they were eager for knowledgeable counsel, and a friend. They wanted to trust someone.

The discussion quickly turned to their son's extradition hearing. Did the professor think Bryan should contest Idaho's attempt to have him return for trial? They had been urging Bryan to oppose the writ; they wanted him close to home for as long as possible. But Bryan disagreed.

He was determined to prove his innocence, and the sooner that happened, then the sooner this entire nightmare would be over.

What do you think, Dr. Ramsland? the Kohbergers asked.

The professor agreed with Bryan. If he was intent on establishing his innocence, then there was no point in putting off that fight. Anyway, she predicted confidently, Idaho would eventually succeed. A legal skirmish would just be postponing the inevitable extradition.

That night the Kohbergers spoke with their son on the phone and conveyed Dr. Ramsland's thoughts. Bryan, his mother told an acquaintance, had seemed very excited that his old professor had reached out to his family.

ON JANUARY 3, SHERIFF'S DEPUTIES led Kohberger into the Monroe County Courthouse for the extradition hearing. A deputy kept firm hold on each of his arms, and he was shackled and handcuffed. He wore a red prison jumpsuit. His parents and two sisters were seated in the visitors' gallery, and as Kohberger shuffled to his seat next to LaBar, he turned toward them. *I love you*, he mouthed silently.

Moments later, LaBar announced that his client would not fight extradition.

Afterward, LaBar released a statement from Kohberger's family. "First and foremost we care deeply for the four families who have lost their precious children," it read. Yet they also wanted it known that they were supportive of their son. "We have fully cooperated with law-enforcement agencies in an attempt to seek the truth and promote his presumption of innocence rather than judge unknown facts and make erroneous assumptions."

LaBar made his feelings clear, too. In a public statement, he sternly lectured, "Mr. Kohberger has been accused of very serious crimes, but the American justice system cloaks him in a veil of innocence . . . He should be presumed innocent until proven otherwise—not tried in the court of public opinion."

———

A DAY LATER, A SLIVER of a moon hanging low in the frigid predawn sky, Kohberger, shackled and still in a red prison jumpsuit, left the prison for the drive to an airport outside Philadelphia. From there he was flown in a tiny fixed wing Pilatus across country. The plane, after a stop for re-fueling, landed at Pullman-Moscow Regional Airport, the same airstrip where only about three weeks earlier Michael Kohberger had arrived in anticipation of a road trip with his son.

Michael, for his part, had spent a large part of that day cleaning up the wreckage that had resulted when the police had stormed into his home. He found cardboard to cover the holes in the broken windows and then affixed strips of duct tape to hold the pieces in place. When he was satisfied, he brought out a shop vacuum to collect the shards of glass that littered the frozen lawn. It was all he could do, he might very well have felt, to repair the destruction that had been caused by his useless loyalty and love.

PART V

THE DEFENSE'S STORY

Kohberger and his lawyer Anne Taylor in court. The defense team labors with the knowledge that their client's life is on the line. *Getty*

TWENTY-NINE

———

Stepping into the courtroom, you know the score. Only one thing matters: getting your client off the hook.

So if the facts are on your side, you pound 'em. If not, pound the table.

Only the more you keep pounding, something unexpected happens. It all comes into focus. Everything starts to make sense.

Because you know it didn't go down the way the prosecution's claiming. There are too many gaps. Too many things don't add up.

And now the facts are on your side, and you're ready to pound the table into smithereens.

And you're staring, eyes as big as saucers, at a premise that'd once seemed impossible: he didn't do it!

Fear commands Bryan Kohberger's defense team—a relentless fear. The three lawyers—all paid by the state of Idaho to represent the suspect and led by Anne Taylor, the cerebral, well-experienced head of the public defender's office up north in Kootenai County—all labor with the knowledge that their client's life is on the line.

In a filing to the court in June 2023, the prosecution had charged that the killings were "especially heinous, atrocious, or cruel" and that the suspect had "exhibited utter disregard for human life." Therefore, the filing went on with sober resolve, "considering all evidence currently known," the state felt "compelled" to seek the death penalty.

Then the stakes were cranked up higher. Weeks later, a state law went into effect ensuring that in the aftermath of the seemingly inevitable guilty verdict in the case, justice would not be deprived of its pound of flesh. If the requisite cocktail of chemicals for a lethal intravenous drip was unavailable, this recently approved statute decreed that a firing squad would be rounded up to get the job done.

With this specter haunting Bryan Kohberger's world, his lawyers have been diligent. They have pounded the courthouse table with motions—a rat-a-tat of demands for discovery, objections to protective orders, even a curious request for the personnel files of three of the cops who played a role in helping to clamp the cuffs on Kohberger.

It was a seemingly desperate strategy, and the authorities paid it little mind. In the second-floor detectives' shack of the Moscow Police Department building, the mood, for a telling example, remained confident. "SODDI," the cops taunted derisively: *Some other dude did it.* Sure, how many times have we heard that and how did those cases work out? We got our man, they insisted, and there's no way he's going to wiggle out of this.

And the facts, as they were enumerated by law enforcement with a prideful confidence, seemed to bolster this argument. For starters—and maybe for finishers, too—there were the fifty-one terabytes of ostensibly confirming data the prosecution had handed over to the defense. They included, according to the court filings, "thousands of pages of discovery, thousands of photographs, hundreds of hours of recordings, many gigabytes of electronic phone records and social media data." And how big was fifty-one terabytes? Well, you might as well be counting the grains of sand on a beach. The sly bottom line was that it would keep the already inundated defense busy for a while, and then some.

But if that was not sufficient to convince the Idaho prison warden to hurry up and get his order in for the chemicals that give the execution hemlock its lethal bite, the local authorities reminded them that they had more aces up their sleeve. For one persuasive item, there was the DNA on the button of the knife sheath found partially under Maddie Mogen. It was a perfect match with a genetic swab of Kohberger's cheek taken shortly after his arrest. For another, there was video of a white Hyundai Elantra similar to the suspect's tearing away from the King Road murder scene in the gray predawn November morning within minutes of when the murders occurred. And for still another, there was the cell phone tower tracking data. Just before 3:00 a.m., as Kohberger left his apartment on the night of the murders, he apparently powered down. Then at nearly 5:00 a.m., about an hour after the killings, his phone sprang back to life just south of Moscow. In a cop's distrustful world where there are no accidents, this timeline was damn incriminating.

The prosecution had even put together a semblance of a motive. It was a neat, two-step argument. First, there was Kohberger's nature: his equilibrium, as revealed by his teenage Internet posts, had always been a balancing act, and a problematic one to boot. "I feel like an organic sack of meat with no self-worth . . . I am starting to view everyone as this," he had, for example, written. Or: "Now I look in the mirror and I see this sickly, tired, useless, and stupid man in the mirror. He is a complete disgrace. He doesn't even deserve to live."

Next, there were the series of shocks that rained down on this fragile stability: the incriminating timeline of his escalating confrontations with his supervising professors in the criminal justice department at WSU. On November 2—eleven days before the King Road murders—he had been hauled before the department bigwigs and informed that he'd better shape up or else. And it was a pretty formidable "or else." If Kohberger couldn't get his act together, behave more professionally in and out of the classroom, then he'd lose his teaching assistant fellowship. Which would also, more consequentially, signal the end of everything to which he had aspired. It would send him sliding back down the ladder he'd been so determinedly climbing since he lost one hundred pounds, kicked heroin, and made up his mind to get a doctorate. He'd be ruined. And if you have nothing, you have nothing to lose. It was the sort of existential jolt that could set demons loose. Or at least, that was one narrative the prosecutors believed they could convincingly spin.

And then there was the clincher. Cop after cop promised that it would be the single unshakable reason Kohberger would be sent by the state to his richly deserved death: Bill Thompson, the county prosecutor. With his long white biblical beard and down-home uniform of jeans and fleece vests, Thompson was a local legend. He had been in office for over thirty years and had famously done the impossible in the closely followed Rachael Anderson murder case, where he won a conviction without the body being found—an improbable victory that sent no less a culprit than a blood relative of Al Capone to jail for life.

Rumor has it that this will be Thompson's last hurrah. There was no way, the cops believed, that he'd retire to idle away his days strumming guitar with his band, the Gefilte Trout (they played rock, folk, country, and even klezmer tunes), and casting his fishing rod without having secured his already impressive reputation with a final victory in a big trial. And trials just don't come any bigger than this in Latah County.

So, people in Moscow will tell you, let the defense file all the Hail Mary motions they want. They're clutching at straws. Case closed. The facts will prevail.

THIRTY

"**B**ad facts" is a phrase defense lawyers like to bandy about. It's a term that's meant to draw an epistemological distinction between what is objectively real and what is subjective opinion. Simply because the prosecutors say it's true, well, that doesn't make it so.

And in Moscow, a supposedly open-and-shut case was starting to loom as a lot more open than shut. At least that's what the defense team had been excitedly whispering to one another, according to several people privy to their deliberations. Give the state's much-vaunted evidence a couple of good swift kicks, and it would break apart.

A litany of doubts had slowly taken a foreboding shape. Consider:

The DNA on the knife-sheath snap? It's "touch" DNA. That is, it was derived from a fingerprint rather than a drop of blood. And that's pretty shaky evidence. The courtroom reality was that in case after case, touch DNA had been tarnished by a motley collection of false-positive results. A smart defense attorney might argue that there was just as much likelihood of touch DNA's being accurate as a juror's winning the lottery. Who'd want to condemn someone to execution based on those odds?

The car videos? There was no image of the driver in any of them, and there was not a single shot that displayed a license plate. *None*. And that meant that there was nothing that definitively put Kohberger at the wheel or demonstrated beyond a reasonable doubt that it was his car. After all, there were a lot of Hyundai Elantras on the road besides Kohberger's. And, adding to the muddle, it had taken the FBI three tries before they'd settled on a vehicle year for the car. There had been a string of miscalculations, and a jury might not be very forgiving.

The cell tower triangulations? Peel away the well-documented limitations of the process, and Kohberger's phone could be placed anywhere within a thirteen-mile radius of the murder house—and that's about as definitive as a suspicion, not a certainty.

The eyewitness identification? Well, a lot of people have bushy eyebrows like the intruder, not just the suspect. Besides, testimony from a witness who was "frozen" and "in shock," as Dylan Mortensen had been bluntly characterized in a police affidavit, would be easy to impugn. Especially by a defense attorney who had bushy eyebrows.

The murder weapon? Where was it? The police had not found the long-bladed knife used in the killings. And so far they had not revealed whether they had been able to establish that Kohberger ever owned such a weapon.

The motive? The timeline narrative the prosecution had been chasing owed as much to clairvoyance as psychology. Speculative psychobabble, at best. And such wispy conjecture would never sway a practical-thinking Idaho jury.

And as for wily Bill Thompson, well, the wags said, the Biden presidency had made one truth uncomfortably clear: "experienced" was just another word for "old."

THE DEFENSE WAS NOW EMBOLDENED. They went on the offensive, and began hammering away at the foundations of the state's argument. And in the process they posed an incendiary question that had the potential to burn the case against Kohberger down to the ground.

What if there was another story out there? the defense asked. Another version of what had happened that night? There were large, lingering mysteries that the prosecution had refused to address. And the defense was now very pointedly working to make the case that these inconvenient truths, when lined up end to end, hinted at another, still-untold story. And that another disturbing possibility existed.

Going back over the events, the timeline for the murders had all along seemed tricky at best. The prosecution had most recently asserted that the killer had done his work in a brutally effective eight minutes, from 4:02 to about 4:10 a.m. Do the grim mathematics and it worked out to an efficient two minutes per victim, and each pair was hunkered down for the night on separate floors. Could a single assassin—a graduate student, not a *sicario*—get the job done with such disciplined professionalism?

Then disappear into the night without leaving a single drop of blood in the house, in his car, on his clothes, or in his apartment? The stunned cops who arrived on the scene had described what they had encountered as "a bloodbath." Was this lack of blood evidence testimony to the killer's fastidiousness, or a prod to go down other ruminative paths?

The coroner had reassured Steve Goncalves that his brave daughter had fought back like a tiger. And yet no traces of cuts, scrapes, or bruises were observed on Kohberger. Four young, fit targets, and he somehow traipsed away with his pasty skin as smooth and unblemished as any sedentary academic's? It didn't seem possible.

And what about the coroner's autopsy reports? What was behind the delay in the determination of Ethan's wounds? The autopsy was performed on November 17, but the report on his death was not issued for nearly a month, on December 15. Had there been a problem in reaching the findings, a final analysis that had been subject to debate?

A further troubling fact: the coroner's description of the wounds (as noted in court documents) seemed to differ from floor to floor in the house. Kaylee and Maddie, lying in the same bed on the third floor, suffered "visible stab wounds." Yet on the floor below, Xana succumbed to "wounds caused by an edged weapon." Ethan's were "caused by sharp-focus injuries." Was there some doubt in the coroner's mind that the wounds were all caused by the same weapon?

But these suspicions were just preludes to the bigger mysteries the defense, no longer passive, was now shouting out loud. In an "Objection to State's Motion for Protective Order," the team zeroed in on several lingering questions. It was a revelatory document—and a provocative one.

It insightfully pointed out that back in the early stages of the case, the prosecution had been made aware of two additional males' DNA found inside the King Road house, as well as male DNA on a glove found outside the residence just days after the murders. If the DNA had been Kohberger's, the prosecution would have been trumpeting this revelation. The state's stony silence, the defense believed, could only mean one thing: the DNA came from three other men. And that left an obvious, yet very pertinent question unanswered: Who are they, and how do these three unknown men fit into the horrific events of that night?

And there was more. The motion dramatically threw a lit match at another powder keg. Quite effectively, it demolished several tantalizing press reports. Forget the fanciful stories about online direct messages between Kohberger and one of the victims. Forget the alleged run-in at a Main Street, Moscow, restaurant where Maddie and Xana had worked. The defense categorically asserted that "there is no connection between Mr. Kohberger and the victims."

And if there was no connection then there was no plausible motive. And without a motive, the random brutal killings of the four college students by a grad student from a nearby university remained an enigma. Why did he do it? There wasn't an answer because the prosecution's story just didn't make sense.

But there was still another mystery at the heart of this case. Namely, the eight-hour gap between when Dylan Mortensen had first heard the disquieting noises in the house—*There's someone here!*—and spotted a masked, black-dressed intruder and when the police were finally summoned. Eight hours! There had been a lot of agile, emphatic explanations offered to explain away this remarkable delay, and none so far, the defense believed, had been satisfactory. Or had the ring of truth.

AND SO THE DEFENSE'S STRATEGY had now taken a new shape, a new direction. The accumulated doubts had worked to liberate them from simply poking holes in the prosecution's case. With this freedom, they began to explore new narratives, alternative versions of what might have happened that fateful night in November on King Road. And if Kohberger wasn't the killer, or if he was an accomplice rather than the sole perpetrator, then they realized they had to go back to what had been previously brushed over. They had to work their way to an explanation that made sense.

And that trail led inexorably to drugs.

THIRTY-ONE

All along it had been hovering in the background. It was the jarring anomaly that largely went unspoken in the squeaky-clean biographies of the four victims that the press had served up. Nevertheless, it was a truth, as regrettable as it was potentially relevant, that three of the victims' parents—Kernodle's mom, Mogen's stepmom, and Mogen's dad—had been arrested on felony drug-possession charges. And even Steve Goncalves could be tarred by a similarly damning brush: his brother Nathan was serving time in jail for a drug-related murder.

From the onset, Anne Taylor, Kohberger's lead legal aid attorney, had been aware of at least some of this history. She had been representing Cara Kernodle before promptly petitioning the court to be removed when offered the bigger challenge of representing the man accused of murdering Kernodle's daughter. In the aftermath, sharp words had been exchanged in the press. Kernodle charged that she had been betrayed; Taylor shot back that she had simply been assigned the case and had never met Kernodle.

Still, four victims and three parents and one uncle with a history of drug arrests? What were the odds? Was it a strange coincidence? A sad commentary on contemporary American life? Or something more telling? Even a clue? In the hectic early days, it had become another of the many stray tidbits that the defense filed away and then promptly forgot. But as the case meandered slowly and tediously through the pretrial stage, a former University of Idaho frat president, a twenty-two-year-old journalism major in his junior year, died not once but twice in a single night. And in the aftermath of his tragic and needless demise, new avenues of speculation multiplied, spreading out in previously unexplored directions.

IT WAS SPRING BREAK, AND Caden Young was looking to score. He succeeded, only to pay with his life. That was the thumbnail history of events as detailed in the initial, terse news stories. But anyone taking the time to go through the voluminous pile of police reports, or conversing with either the detective who had caught the case or, equally elucidating, the legal aid lawyer who subsequently became involved, would latch on to a richer account. And one that added two new actors to the drama. They were a couple who quickly caught the Kohberger defense team's rapt attention.

The penultimate day of Young's brief life began with a decision to leave the apartment in Centralia, Washington, where he was visiting a onetime Alpha Kappa Lambda fraternity brother, Christopher O'Flaherty. After O'Flaherty had left for work, Young decided he'd take an Uber to Tacoma, where he would meet up with some friends who would drive him to Seattle. The next morning, at nearly 1:00 a.m., O'Flaherty, as he recalled the building drama, got a call from Young announcing that he was in the Harborview Hospital, in Seattle, and needed a lift home.

"Bro, what happened?" O'Flaherty asked with concern.

Young, with a matter-of-factness that left his friend astonished, recounted that he'd been partying that afternoon with friends in a room at a Seattle Holiday Inn and had snorted lines of cocaine apparently laced with fentanyl. Within moments his face went white, then blue, and suddenly everything turned completely black. "I was dead, bro," was how Young, still dazed and bewildered by it all, explained with a hapless resignation.

An ambulance, however, had been summoned. Naloxone was administered. And the next thing Young remembered was waking up in a bed in the hospital. Alive. He was now being released, and he was hoping his old Alpha Kappa brother would come and get him.

At 2:00 a.m., O'Flaherty made his way to the hospital and retrieved his buddy. On the ride back to Centralia, he grew concerned because his passenger seemed "out of it," nodding off frequently. But they nevertheless stopped at a Jack in the Box to grab burgers; Young had roused from his fog long enough to announce in an imploring voice that he was hungry.

Once back at O'Flaherty's apartment, though, Young promptly crashed on the futon in his friend's bedroom. And he was snoring something awful. O'Flaherty playfully recorded the racket on his phone; he thought they'd have a good laugh over it in the morning. But when he checked on his friend a bit later, there was a swirl of whitish vomit circling Caden's mouth, and a frantic search for a pulse revealed nothing. When the medics arrived, it became official: Caden had suffered his second and final death.

It was all too common—another young life ravaged by fentanyl—and within days it might very well have become another dreadful statistic in a national body count that was climbing toward pandemic proportions. But then the police made two arrests in connection with Young's death.

HURRYING TO ROOM 214 OF the Holiday Inn where Young had first overdosed, the police arrested Emma Bailey, twenty-two, of Moscow and Demetrius Robinson, thirty-six, of Tacoma just as the couple were about to leave. They were each charged with one count of conspiracy to commit a violation of the Uniform Controlled Substance Act—that is, they had allegedly supplied the student with lethal fentanyl-laced cocaine—and held on $100,000 bail. Pleading not guilty, but unable to post bail, they were shuffled off to the Lewis County jail.

The pair spent two months and five days behind bars, and during that time law-enforcement investigators and the press kept digging. And what they unearthed grabbed the attention of the Kohberger defense team.

Robinson—or D, as he was widely known in the college towns of both Moscow, Idaho, and Pullman, Washington—had a dismaying rap sheet. "Extensive" was the adjective the local paper used to describe it. "Violent" was the modifier, though, that leaped up in the minds of the defense investigators.

Among the eyebrow-raising highlights: a fifteen-month prison sentence for second-degree assault in Pullman back in 2018; a second-degree rape investigation two years later; and then, in 2001, an arrest in Pullman for suspicion of possession of a controlled substance with intent to deliver, and for allegedly assaulting a companion when their alleged partnership went south. While the drug case had fallen apart because of legal concerns provoked by an overly gungho search of a hotel room, the fourth-degree harassment charges stuck, and he served 151 days in jail. Also scattered about Robinson's sheet were five charges for driving with a suspended license, one of which landed him in jail for five days; there was an outstanding arrest warrant for another.

As for Bailey, her record was more banal: a DUI arrest after she breezed through a red light in Pullman around 2:00 a.m. (There was an unintentionally amusing visual record of the aftermath: a police body-cam video of an obviously inebriated, yet indignant, Emma trying with impressive sincerity to convince the bemused cop that she hadn't been out seriously drinking.)

Bailey's mother, Kimberley, though, told a more plaintive and complicated story about her daughter in two lengthy telephone conversations that were recorded by the Centralia detectives investigating the sale of the lethal fentanyl-laced cocaine. As the mother shared the tale, her daughter was an innocent Moscow High graduate who had put in a disjointed year at the University of Idaho before hooking up with Robinson, fourteen years her senior, a charmer with his cornrows and tough-guy menace. And what a tumultuous five-year love story their romance had been!

Bailey, her mother said, had allegedly been living in fear of Robinson's violent mood swings and hair-raising threats of what would happen to her family if she ever left him. There had been times, in fact, when Kimberley and her ex-husband had rushed to their daughter's rescue after getting a teary distress call. They'd drive for hours and then covertly ferry Emma off while Robinson was sleeping the afternoon away. But each time, Bailey would run back to Robinson.

And there was more. When the cops dug deeper, they grew to suspect that the couple were very possibly dealing drugs they'd scored in Seattle to the local colleges in Pullman and Moscow. The detective's incident report flatly stated, "There were investigations in other jurisdictions for Emma and Demetrius for narcotics trafficking."

O'Flaherty told the cops that he'd first met Bailey when she'd come to Alpha Lambda Kappa parties to see if the brothers were interested in scoring some coke. He soon learned firsthand, however, that she was merely the engaging go-between. Robinson was the iron-fisted closer. He'd hand over the product and give you a look that made sure you paid. And this frat-boy account was not an outlier. Talk to students and ex-students in Moscow and Pullman who knew Bailey and Robinson and the response was a uniform chorus: the couple did a lively business dealing drugs along Greek Row.

Tanner Aspire, though, offered a different perspective. He was, he announced with an obvious pride, "D's good buddy" and was planning to go into business with him. The business? Fish-farming, although the location was still up in the air. Colorado, or then again, maybe Montana. The goal, he explained, was to sell trout throughout the entire Midwest.

But all his airy business talk was just a prelude to the message he wanted to deliver. "Both Emma and D . . . would never deal drugs. And they never sold any cocaine to Caden." He added with an unwavering conviction, "The worst you can say is that D has an anger-management problem. But D is getting it under control."

"It's a real love story," he went on with force. "Where D goes, Emma goes."

And the couple did in fact go off together. Just five days before the trial for supplying the lethal cocaine was to begin, a judge dismissed the case. Their legal aid lawyer had zeroed in on a technicality, but it was a very consequential one: "the question of prosecutorial jurisdiction." Apparently they'd been scheduled to be tried in the county where the death had occurred, rather than where the cocaine had been originally ingested.

But their good fortune might be short-lived. The judge had dismissed the case "without prejudice." That meant that it could be refiled in the same court of law if the authorities drafted a new and more carefully drawn indictment.

Was one in the works? All a Centralia detective who'd been involved in the case from the morning he'd found Young's inert body would pointedly say was, "We're not going to let this case disappear."

And the detective was not alone. The case had not disappeared from the thoughts of the Kohberger defense team, either. It became the shovel the team used to dig deep into the possibility of narcotics trafficking along Greek Row. And the more they dug, the more they began to wonder with a hardening focus whether these furtive activities had played a part in four murders.

THIRTY-TWO

The defense investigators' first stop was the Seattle DEA field office. And the overview they offered was by all accounts a tale of cutthroat international intrigue. It was the story of a pipeline that ran from China, where the fentanyl precursor chemicals were produced, to the sinister Sinaloa and Jalisco Cartels in Mexico, which manufactured the drugs and then smuggled the too-often-lethal product to their distribution networks in northwestern urban hubs such as Seattle and Spokane. Next, with the eager help of a freelance army of small-time distributors, the drugs reached into the seemingly wholesome all-American counties and college towns—like Moscow, Idaho.

That was the view from a thousand feet. But Sheriff Brett Myers, head of the Quad Cities Drug Task Force, a multijurisdictional team propped up, in part, by federal money, whose territory included the university towns of Moscow and Pullman (along with Lewis-Clark State College in Lewiston, Idaho), offered a ground-level account. And it was enough to give anyone whose child was heading off to college in the area the willies.

The sheriff shared that his task force was "working with college kids" in the local schools whom they had caught dealing MDMA and cocaine, "flipping them," and then using the students "to go after the big local dealers." And once the scared-witless college kids had helped his team ID the foot soldiers, "we go up the ladder to get the people tied to the cartels in the cities."

The sheriff took a philosophical perspective on the possible danger the frat-boy double agents might be heading into. "It could be," he acknowledged equably. "There are some very tough guys running this business." The risks, however, were no deterrent. "We're game to do that every day of the week," he promised.

Was some sort of similar intrigue going on in Moscow the night the four students were murdered? The sheriff was not involved in the investigation and therefore can only speculate. But his was a local lawman's informed conjecture. And a resonating one: "Could it have been a drug-related case? I can't rule it out. It's not improbable. From what I know, that'd answer a lot of questions."

DID ANY OF THE VICTIMS know Emma Bailey and Demetrius Robinson? Had the couple from time to time joined the throng of kids who regularly flocked to the King Road house? Those now became the game-changing questions the investigators for the defense have been trying to answer.

Follow their winding path:

Ashlin Couch had been one of the original signers of the lease on the King Road house with the others, but she had never moved in. Nevertheless, she remained a friend, as well as a sorority sister, of several of the residents, and, according to some reports, she would visit from time to time. She even celebrated her twenty-first birthday with a spirited party at King Road.

And Couch followed Bailey on Instagram. Which could mean something. Or nothing.

But it did lead the defense team to another even more pertinent question: Did Bailey know Kohberger?

This inquiry, one that had the potential to turn the entire case inside out, persuaded investigators to revisit Kohberger's first day in Moscow—the pool party at The Grove. They realized it was suddenly necessary to look deep into the festivities from a previously ignored perspective.

IN THE FRENETIC DAYS FOLLOWING the arrest, a team of FBI agents had grandly commandeered a room at the redbrick Lightly Student Services building on the main WSU campus. And with a professional politeness that won over even the most belligerent student, they began interviewing anyone who knew Kohberger. In the process, they dutifully had inquired if anyone had any photos or even a video from that summer's pool party at The Grove.

A few pieces of evidence were produced. It was not an extensive record of the day—more a haphazard collection of snapshots and at least one brief, somewhat random cell phone video. The agents had been searching for sightings of Goncalves, Mogen, Kernodle, or Chapin, trying to discover something, anything, that could tie Kohberger to the victims.

They could not find the faces of any of the four students in the material. Which meant that they weren't at The Grove pool party. Or they simply didn't appear in the photos that were taken that day. Or, no less likely, maybe they just weren't in the handful that were shared with the bureau.

But now the defense was wondering: What if the FBI's review, done in the early, uninformed days of the investigation, had been too narrow? What if they had scrutinized the photos and the video and had ignored the possible presence of another guest whose appearance could put a new spin on what had happened at the house on King Road?

What if Emma Bailey had been at the pool party?

If she had been, then she might very well have been approached by a Kohberger on the make, same as the two young women in the black bikinis. And if, as the police allege, she was in the habit of dealing recreational drugs, it might have been a connection a onetime heroin addict like Kohberger would have relished. It might have been an association that, unlike his approaches to the other two female partygoers, could have had some longevity. In fact, he might even have visited Bailey from time to time at her home in Moscow, which, as it happened, was tucked into the very end of a cul-de-sac a minute or so drive away from the murder house. Which would put it very much within the same incriminating cell tower radius as the scene of the crime on King Road.

It was a tantalizing hypothesis, and its significance only gained power in the wake of a new motion the defense had filed: Kohberger has an alibi.

"Evidence corroborating Mr. Kohberger being at a location other than the King Road address will be disclosed," Anne Taylor wrote in a court filing. Yet with a dramatist's flair, she held on to her punch line. She did not reveal any further details. Presumably, all will be disclosed at the trial.

But for now, the defense's motion makes one already heady question even more relevant: Was Emma at the party?

Seven people who were there were queried, and the responses—all shared after a good deal of thought—ran the narrow gamut from "I think she was" to "She might have been."

But no one said she definitely was. And no one said she definitely wasn't. In short, there remained enough for the defense to offer a hypothetical alternative to the version of events that will be rolled out by the prosecution.

Or at least that is what the defense is hoping. Yet these speculations—when held up to the light—immediately turned porous. There was never any drug paraphernalia found in the house. And while the complete autopsy reports on the four victims have not been released, there has been no claim that drugs were found in any of them at the time of their deaths. And as for Emma Bailey and Demetrius Robinson, no one has constructed an airtight case that they were ever involved in any sort of drug deals with any of the residents of King Road. Or, for that matter, that they had ever entered the house.

Ultimately, with the death penalty hovering portentously over the proceedings, it will come down to two conflicting stories. And it will all be left to the jury to make sense of it all. And at the conclusion of a trial, suspicions might weigh as heavily as facts in the minds of the jury when they need to decide if one more life should be taken in retribution for the four that were already extinguished.

THE JURY. IN A HEARTLAND community such as Moscow, the predilection for Old Testament, eye-for-eye justice would, the defense presumed, rule. Despite the many deficiencies in the narrative, they feared, the prosecution would nevertheless not need to work too hard to spin a scenario that would send Kohberger to death row.

Or at least that's what they had thought until they began weighing the disproportionate influence Doug Wilson's Christ Church parishioners had on the jury pool. About two thousand or so strong, the Kirkers, as the church members called themselves, amounted perhaps to half of the town's non-university-affiliated jury pool. And here's what left the defense team's hopes surging: the church, as personified by Wilson, was in a state of war with the town authorities—including the police department, whose investigation had built the case against Kohberger.

Just days before Kohberger's arrest, Wilson had shared his prickly feelings about the town fathers in one of the weekly encyclicals that he sent to his flock. "Our local city government, law enforcement included, is a nest of incompetence and corruption," he told the church members. Refusing to turn the other cheek, he went on with a measured force: "If the additional scrutiny over the murder case is part of what brings about a much-needed house cleaning, then we should be grateful for that—but without any unlawful gloating."

The roots of this church-state animosity stem from the several police arrests and subsequent lawsuits local officials have filed against Christ Church parishioners (including Wilson's son and his two grandsons, one now a student at Columbia University) for a maskless public pray-in during the pandemic and a few stickers protesting coronavirus restrictions that had been affixed to a town lamppost.

"You'd think we'd be a natural constituency for 'back the blue,' but after what we have experienced, I think that if any of my parishioners are on the jury, I'd tell them to go in with an open mind," Wilson asserted.

But the reverend's own mind was not that open. If a Moscow cop were to testify against Kohberger, he has warned, his parishioners would have reason to be skeptical. "After all, we know their officers have lied on the stand before," he explained, referring to the cases involving his son and grandsons.

And Wilson did not flinch from making his way to what was now the bottom legal line of the Moscow murders. "From what I've read, there are a lot of questions that still need to be answered.

"I think it's very possible the prosecution has the wrong man," he warned.

PART VI

STEVE'S STORY

Kristi and Steve Goncalves. For them, "Justice for Kaylee" meant that their daughter's killer would face a firing squad. *KHQ*

THIRTY-THREE

————

People say time heals all wounds. They tell you you'll get over it.
But they've never buried their child.
That stays with you. It works on you. It sinks in deep and never
lets go.
Solace? Not a chance.
But still you try. You discover anger. You vow vengeance.
But it doesn't help, and you know it. It's not enough.
It's the armor you've put on to keep from constantly screaming.

What was Steve Goncalves to make of all this? If he allowed himself simply to be led by his broken heart, then he could sit back, breathe a comforting sigh of relief, and rejoice that the authorities had gotten their man. He could at last hope to find a measure of peace.

Or could he? For as events unexpectedly began to play out, the arrest brought him neither a sense of resignation nor one of acceptance. And most certainly not calm. Instead, new nagging questions arose, and in their wake new resentments flourished. Time to think, Steve was learning, was always dangerous.

The stories about an extraordinary courtroom upset in the making had made their way to him, too. And as he followed what he was hearing about the case the defense had been so assiduously building, as he scoured the Internet and discovered a rabble of often-intriguing theories, he grew concerned. It was a world of startling new information; if he stood still, the case would pass him by. He felt assailed.

And soon it was as if his old anger, his often-shared doubts about the competence of the police, their half measures and failures, had never left. All his old suspicions had broken loose and risen up in him once more. And to do nothing would be a betrayal of his steely vow: "I'm telling you right now, we're coming for you."

Yet, it wasn't simply vanity, the belief that one middle-aged guy with only a background in IT could get to the bottom of things. Rather, he explained to a friend, it was, in part, a new red-hot anger that propelled him forward. He was furious that the trial had been postponed indefinitely; the prosecution's latest cavalier suggestion was that the proceedings should take place when the local high school was not in session to ensure that the anticipated courthouse traffic wouldn't interfere with the school buses, but whether that meant this summer or the next remained anybody's guess. And making the delay even more unconscionable, Steve felt, was the draconian gag order that severely limited what the law-enforcement authorities, the lawyers, and the families of the victims could publicly say about the case. It was not just that he deemed this restriction a violation of his fundamental constitutional rights. Rather, the paucity of reputable intelligence had created a vacuum that's been filled by rumors, half-truths, and crackpot lies.

Steve needed answers, not rumors. And he was sedulous. He remained determined to make sure the authorities had arrested the right man. This, he confided to a friend he had reached out to in his despair, was a large part of what kept him up at night, staring sleepless at the ceiling. For while he had grown increasingly convinced that Kohberger was involved in the crime, Steve remained open to the possibility, he had explained, that there were more perpetrators in the house on King Road on the night his daughter and her friends were killed.

And with this possibility, a new dread took hold—a rising consternation that if he waited passively for the cops finally to share what they had managed to uncover, it might be too late. The remaining unidentified perpetrators—if they did indeed exist—would have escaped.

AND SO ALTHOUGH MORE THAN a year had passed since the arrest of Bryan Kohberger in Pennsylvania, Steve had plowed on. It had not been an easygoing adventure, or always fruitful. Early on, for a cruel example, an enticing tip came his way from a source he described in a text he sent to a friend as "a jailhouse snitch." It was a convict's tale, something supposedly overheard in the prison yard, that offered to tie up all the loose ends of the case. Spurred on by that promise, both Steve and the private detective he had hired fanned out with their inquiries into several states. Steve was energized by the possibility that he was on the verge of accomplishing what the professionals had failed to do: he'd get the whole story.

But after an exhausting, time-consuming probe, it was clear it had been nothing more than an elaborate con, a malicious scheme to squeeze some money out of a grieving family's misery. The experience was demoralizing.

Yet Steve persevered, only to be conned again. A grainy lightbulb cam video of the King Road neighborhood came his way that proved Kohberger wasn't the lone killer. It was only after he went to considerable expense and hired a professional videographer to examine the recording that he conceded it was a fake.

Then there was his decision to leak a time-stamped video of another vehicle tearing away from the street adjacent to the murder house just before dawn on the morning of November 13 to one of the true-crime Internet sites. His logic was that it was very possibly significant evidence; it needed widespread scrutiny. But this video, too, was also ultimately deemed irrelevant, and in the end his tangential role in its dissemination became an embarrassment.

All of this folly brought Steve to two unwavering conclusions.

One: theories suggesting that a drug ring had been involved were ludicrous. "No pro is going to rough up someone not knowing who all is in the house," he texted one of the new confederates he had befriended while looking for knowledgeable allies on the Internet. There were, he pointed out, usually only three girls in the King Road house; his daughter, who had completed all her coursework and would graduate in January, had just come down to Moscow for the weekend on a whim to show Maddie her new Range Rover. "Explain to me how a hit man missed Ethan and Kaylee's new car." A professional, he argued, would have been daunted by the presence of two additional people in the house.

As for the rumors of a drug deal gone bad being the underlying motive, Steve considered it a nonstarter. Although the complete autopsy had not been released, he had been told by the authorities that the toxicity reports on all four of the victims established that they had no drugs in their systems. Besides, if they'd wanted to score some pot, there was no need to get involved with a street dealer. "The kids," he objected, "could go down a street and in eight miles there was a store" where they could easily make a buy (despite the fact that marijuana remained illegal in Idaho). "Kristi [his wife] went with them once to check it out," he texted to his new confidant.

Two: "there are some crazy-ass people who are really crazy" who were trying to elbow their way into the case with deliberate misinformation.

BUT NOT ALL OF STEVE'S investigative efforts have been in vain. He had assembled some blue-chip sources that, he revealed to several friends, included an FBI agent in the St. Louis office, who had shared his personal email so that his bosses in the bureau wouldn't learn that he was communicating with Steve; a handful of additional sympathetic law enforcement officers; and, most helpful of all, a conduit to two of the grand jurors who had been on the panel that had voted to indict Bryan Kohberger. And in the process, he had compiled some startling revelations, hard-won information that he triumphantly disclosed to his newfound Internet associates:

Kohberger had purchased a dark blue Dickies long-sleeved work uniform at the Walmart in Pullman, Washington, not long before the murders, Steve had learned. The authorities had a copy of the $49.99 receipt, and they also now had a theory to explain how Kohberger had managed to escape from the crime scene without a scratch and without leaving an incriminating drop of blood in his getaway car or his apartment: he had worn the work uniform during the murders, and then had disrobed before he got behind the wheel of his Hyundai Elantra for his circuitous drive back to his apartment. Perhaps, the authorities hypothesized, he had stuffed the work suit into a plastic garbage bag and then shoved it into his trunk.

Only there was no sign of the Dickies outfit. The police had looked high and low, but they couldn't find it, just as they couldn't locate the murder weapon. It was rumored in the press that they had a receipt for a Ka-Bar knife he had purchased online, months before the killings, but as for the actual knife, it, too, had seemingly vanished. And as long as these two crucial pieces of evidence remained unavailable, Steve could only wonder with a swelling apprehension what a jury would make of their absence.

Even more troubling, if true, was what Steve had learned from people who had spoken to members of the grand jury who had been presented with the prosecution's case. It centered on the alleged behavior of the two roommates who had miraculously survived the night unscathed. How, he had long wondered, could they have slept, blissfully unaware, in the aftermath of the savage predawn stabbing murders of four of their friends in a narrow house with paper-thin walls?

Now he had an answer—perhaps. Steve had been told that the two survivors allegedly had not only been awake while the killings had taken place but that they had heard everything. More astonishingly, his grand-jury sources alleged that the two girls had been texting each other as the murderer methodically went from one room to the next.

The possibility that two people had a sense of the horror while it occurred and had not acted, calling neither friends nor 911, left Steve floored. No less confounding, they had, if his sources were as knowledgeable as he believed, then let hour after hour after hour tick away before they finally decided to summon friends. It added an entirely new band of mystery to a crime that was encircled by so many unanswered questions.

In the aftermath of this startling intelligence, Steve felt he had no choice but to intensify his efforts. And in that dogged process, he came to believe that the government must have a protected source, an informant who could provide testimony that would tighten the screws that held together the case against Kohberger. Steve was determined to talk to this individual. He did not want to wait for a distant trial to get the knowledge he needed. For his peace of mind, he needed relief now.

And after some digging, he grew convinced he had the informant in his sights. He was preparing to reach out to this individual, to get right in his face and confront him. He would explain that he was empowered by a father's natural right to understand fully the last moments of his daughter's life. It was his duty. This was an argument, he felt, that no one could reject. At last he would know the whole story of what had really happened to Kaylee. And why.

But before he could make his move, before he could get in a room and have a heart-to-heart talk with the witness, he was unexpectedly stopped in his tracks—by the FBI.

The bureau, Steve informed people, had sent an official letter to his attorney in Moscow, Shanon Gray, warning that if there were any attempts to contact the individual Steve had been pursuing, there would be legal consequences. The witness had originally reached out to the authorities through a tip line that promised to protect the identities of anyone volunteering information, and the bureau had to honor that commitment. Further, the letter made clear with an intimidating fixity, the fact that Steve was the father of one of the victims gave him no dispensation from the legal consequences that accompany tampering with a government witness.

Stymied, Steve skulked away. The promise of a real understanding was out there, yet still beyond his grasp. Racked by frustration and despair, all he could do was send a disheartened text to one of his fellow Internet detectives: "There is so much more to this than is in the media."

MEMORIES ARE DRAWN FROM THE past. Dreams, however, are part of an idealized vision of what the world might become. They hold the future.

And now thwarted in his sleuthing, still staring with bitterness at hard mysteries he cannot crack, Steve has expanded his focus. Driven by memories of his daughter, he has found an alternative summons. A call to another sort of action. If he cannot conduct the investigation he feels he must, then he will at least ensure that at some distant appointed time there will be a measure of justice.

On the Goncalves Family Page on Facebook, Steve, his wife, and his daughter Alivea, along with other relatives, appear in hoodies displaying a stony message: #JUSTICEFORKAYLEE, HOUSE BILL 186, SHOTS FIRED. The Idaho State Legislature Bill 186, passed last March after Kohberger's indictment, affirmed that if the chemicals required for an intravenous execution were unavailable, a death sentence could be fulfilled by a firing squad.

It was an unforgiving promise, and Steve had pledged his support. And with this allegiance, he had become another victim, another innocent sucked down into the swirling vortex of the hostile, destructive force that had been set loose in the aftermath of that terrible November night in Moscow.

His future was now a raging, all-consuming anger.

EPILOGUE

The University of Idaho ordered that the murder house on King Road be demolished—only to learn that bulldozers cannot eradicate the past. *(Associated Press)*

Why is beyond your reach. It's an equation that can't be solved. An atom that can't be split.

There will never be an answer that makes sense.

And without this knowledge, without the exculpation of reason or faith or purpose that understanding can offer, things will not hold together.

Gravity has failed, and you're forever falling.

Even the murder house has been destroyed. The university gave the order, and it was swiftly leveled to the ground. Not a trace of it remains. A flat, dark tract has replaced it.

And the trial? Postponed, and then postponed again. And so now after all the tedious, exasperating delays, whenever it finally does take place, it will be a footnote to the larger, ineluctable events. The damage has already been done.

Besides, what will the trial reveal? The dialectics of the courtroom would inevitably prevail and opposing teams of experts will be summoned to go at one another. For every expert who solemnly testifies the cell phone tower evidence is irrefutable, another will be produced to refute it. For every scientist who makes sweeping, unwavering claims about the touch DNA on the button snap of the knife sheath, there will be another, equally sincere, equally well credentialed, to insist that it is a conjuror's trick. For every deep analysis of the surveillance videos of a white Hyundai Elantra racing through the first light of dawn, there will be another that insists it's a murky, indecipherable wash. For every expert, there will be a counterauthority. And in the end, the jury will need to wade through what will certainly be a series of near-impenetrable disputes and somehow make a reasonable decision.

I AM ASSAILED BY ALL these thoughts as I return to the scene of the crime. I am standing on a ridge on Greek Row and I can look down sharply toward King Road and see the vacant lot where the infamous house once stood. It grows dark early in the first days of spring in Idaho, and my recognition that the night has started falling triggers a memory of the last time I stood on this spot.

It had been a cold night late in December. The sky was gray, heavy with the promise of snow, and just moments earlier I had been only yards or so away from the front door of the pale, flat-colored house at 1122 King Road. The street had been impossibly still; there were no extraneous sounds that night. I tried to imagine the house as it was in one of the bodycam videos the Moscow cops had released, when it had been something vibrant and energetic.

Suddenly, I had been trapped in a very bright cone of fierce white light.

I was taken by surprise—stunned, in fact. And my first startled, terrified thought: This was what it must have been like to have been awakened without warning from a deep sleep. And to find yourself staring at someone raising a knife. *There's someone here!*

Then I heard a voice. "You gotta be careful there. It's icy."

A black security vehicle had been parked kitty-corner to the front door of the house, the car concealed by the dark shadows. And the officer at the wheel, I now realized, had illuminated the auxiliary spotlight mounted on his door, pinning me in its harsh glare.

"Thanks, Officer," I answered. "I'll take care."

And I headed off, walking absently in the darkness out of the gulch and moving uphill. In the raw cold, my dark stocking cap pulled low on my forehead, my hands shoved deep in the pockets of my parka, I found myself standing on a flat, grassy ridge on Nez Perce Drive. It was adjacent to the fraternity house where Ethan and Xana had partied on their last night together. And then the snow had started to fall in big, thick silver flakes.

From my vantage point, I could look down at the house on King Road and watched as the snow began to cover it. The same falling snow that I imagined blanketing the old redbrick university buildings, the roads that twisted through the humpbacked northern Idaho hills. And the final resting places of the four dead students.

And at that moment, watching the snow thickly descend, I had a premonition: Soon everything will be concealed. And everything will be forgotten.

It's nearly eighteen months later and I have returned to this ridge and I realize how terribly wrong I was.

For it's as if I can still feel the demons that were unleashed swirling about, wild and devious. Encircling me. This is a drama not just about victims, but also about the victimized. They have lost their sanity, their wisdom, their love, and their faith. It is a story, I fear, where there are no survivors. Nothing has changed. And nothing ever will.

YET AS I STAND THERE, there still remains, I realize, one question. And it is the most perplexing: Why? Why would anyone—Kohberger? A drug-crazed assassin? A psychopath on the prowl?—take it upon himself to kill four young, exuberant, attractive students? Sure, the prosecutors will diligently try to stitch together a motive because that's what they know they need to do.

They will look for logic, for reason, but those are benchmarks that are not applicable to this madness.

So why?

A killer, I believe, needs only two things: someone to love, and someone to hate.

Did the killer love the kids on King Road, fantasize about their beauty and ebullience, and hate himself for his inability to be what they were?

Or did the killer hate the victims, hate the way their images marched through his mind, and love himself so excessively that he had no choice but to rid the world of their rebuking presence?

We will likely never know. And it is folly to think otherwise.

NEVERTHELESS, I SUSPECT I KNOW what happened.

Bryan Kohberger was, I believe, the murderer. And while, I concede, it might be possible to impugn specific items of evidence, when wedged together each fits neatly with the others to form a coherent and very persuasive whole. The DNA evidence from the cheek swab, the car videos, the knife purchase receipt the authorities have found, the cell phone tower pings, Kohberger's sorting his personal garbage into plastic bags and depositing it into a Pennsylvania neighbor's trash can—any one of these items might be seen as specious or even a coincidence, but when assembled with one another they coalesce into an overwhelming argument for guilt.

I also believe his target was Maddie Mogen, and her alone. Why? When he entered the house through the second-floor sliding door off the kitchen, the killer immediately headed to the third floor—to Maddie's bedroom. If he had been simply intent on killing everyone in the house, he would have started his savagery on the second floor.

He had no knowledge that Kaylee had returned for the weekend to show off her new car, or that he would find her in Maddie's bedroom. And he only encountered Ethan after he had descended to the second floor. Yet once Xana overheard the encounter and spoke up, she, too, was doomed. Kaylee, Xana, and Ethan—they all were grim collateral damage. The killer needed to escape, and they were in his way.

But what about Dylan? How does one explain her passive behavior, as well as the killer's decision to spare her life? I think the only reasonable explanation is one that defies commonplace reason: they both were in parallel states of shock, both locked so tight into their own private worlds—a young girl's terror; a killer's mania—that they could not see beyond the moments they were living through at the time. They both had fallen into a void where no one else could enter. If Dylan had spoken up, as Ethan and Xana had, if she had attempted to penetrate the killer's armory of hate, I believe she would have been another victim.

And as I see that night unfolding in my mind's eye, I have little doubt that the killer acted alone. A scenario that involved multiple assailants would have left more DNA evidence, other cars would have been captured on surveillance videos leaving the scene of the crime, and other cell phones would have been recorded pinging off the nearby towers. And, also likely, by now another, more straightforward—and, paradoxically, more reasonable—motive would have leaked and taken a convincing shape. But this was not a transactional or pragmatic crime.

It happened, I imagine, like this: Kohberger had crossed paths with Maddie, most likely at the Mad Greek restaurant on Main Street in Moscow, which offered the sort of vegan dishes he preferred and where she was a waitress. Did they talk? Did he ask her out? There is no evidence of any significant interaction. And, I believe, one wasn't necessary for her image to take hold of his thoughts. Obsessions came easily to him; he only believed deeply. I suspect that after their initial encounter, however fleeting and slight, he continued to follow her over many nights. And while the roommates hosted party after party at the house on King Road, he was often watching from the shadows.

Yet I do not believe that he was casing the house on his three trips to the neighborhood in the hours after midnight on November 13. Each one was, I contend, a killer's journey—only he could not find the will necessary to step across the barrier that existed between the idea and the reality. After each trip, he wanted to run away, to return to his apartment. A violent battle must have been raging inside his head as he tried with an increasing desperation to fight off the demons that told him his role in life was to get revenge on all the people he could never be like. He was wavering, and he needed to become completely convinced that he deserved what they had, and therefore anything was justifiable, before he could act. And he needed to hear the voices telling him that he was smarter than everyone else: he could get away with murder.

IS THIS WHAT REALLY HAPPENED? We may not know for certain. And as I stand on this grassy ridge struggling to make some sense of it all, my thoughts are interrupted by the loud, blaring sound of rock music. I look up and I see that the door of one of the fraternity houses has swung open as a couple, a young man and his date, enter. They are holding hands, and smiling with a shared, giddy intimacy. For some reason, the door remains opened, and, along with the music, the thick sounds of a party, joyful and promising, lift across the night. I hesitate, but then hurry off toward it before the door closes shut.

ACKNOWLEDGMENTS

We were sitting around the Thanksgiving table two years ago when the talk turned to the perplexing murders of four college students that had occurred not much more than a week earlier in Moscow, Idaho. This was not as strange as it might seem; the grim event had been all over the news, and by that point in the long-running meal we had, full of despair, exhausted the old standby of politics.

As I listened to the conversation, I grew increasingly fascinated; previously I had not paid too much attention to the barrage of daily news stories detailing the tragedy. But now I realized that there was so much that remained unknown—four young deaths, and no sign of a motive or, for that matter, any clue that might lead to a suspect. It was a real-life mystery, and it was just beginning to unfold. And over the long holiday weekend that followed, I, someone who has measured out his professional life by chasing down intriguing, puzzling stories, decided that I wanted to head off to Moscow, Idaho, and see what I could discover.

Sunday afternoon I sent off emails to the two editors/cofounders of *Air Mail*, a wide-ranging, yet always compelling, online weekly for which I had been writing. I asked not only whether they would be interested in a piece on the case, but also (more boldly, arguably) whether they'd be willing to foot the not-insignificant bill for my travel. And I amended this request with what undoubtedly was not a very reassuring caveat: I was not at all certain that I would return from this cross-country trip with a story worth publishing. I very well might get nowhere.

Nevertheless, to my great delight, both Graydon Carter (who had been my editor at *Vanity Fair*) and Alessandra Stanley (whose career at the *New York Times* had overlapped a bit with my years at the paper) responded the next morning with enthusiasm: Book your ticket. And so within a couple of days I was traipsing down the frigid, snow-covered streets of Moscow.

As things worked out, I would make several more trips to Idaho (as well as to Pennsylvania and Washington State) over the next year for *Air Mail* as I researched this story. And over the course of the next fourteen months, I wrote six lengthy pieces on the case for that publication—all of them not just encouraged by Graydon and Alessandra, but also influenced and shaped by their wise comments. Ash Carter did the laborious editing of the pieces, and he was a godsend—perceptive, thoughtful, diligent, and all while working against a looming weekly deadline. This book would never have been written without their initial support and continuing guidance, and I am deeply grateful to each of them.

Then, as my *Air Mail* articles started to appear, I began to mull the possibility that there was a larger story to tell, a fuller nonfiction narrative that could be constructed—and that this ambition required the scope of a book. I turned immediately to my longtime agent and friend Lynn Nesbit and, as she has done for decades, she expertly guided me through the process of finding a home for this proposed work. In truth, I owe my career as an author to Lynn, and, no less important, her friendship has been one of the blessings in my life. And as we moved forward, once again Mina Hamedi at Janklow & Nesbit proved invaluable.

To my great delight, Jonathan Burnham, the publisher of the Harper Group, which had been the home to my previous five books, was immediately interested. He's someone who actually reads the books he publishes, and so it's always a pleasure to work with him. And also on board was

Jonathan Jao, who had smartly edited my last three books. But just as I started writing, Jonathan moved on to an exalted position at another publisher and I was suddenly confronted with the daunting prospect of having to work on a complicated book on an onerous timetable with a new editor, someone that, to boot, I had not previously known.

As things worked out, I sure got lucky. Sean Desmond was just the editor I—and this book—needed. Working against a seemingly impossible deadline, he somehow managed to peruse every sentence with attention and expertise. And the comments and insights he offered were invaluable. He made my book better, and I'm very grateful. I'm also appreciative of the work at HarperCollins done on my book's behalf by David Howe, Tom Hopke, and Tina Andreadis, all valued colleagues from past books. In addition, Trina Hunn's careful reading of an early draft of the manuscript perceptively guided me through potential minefields.

And even as I was writing, Hollywood expressed interest in the forthcoming book. The complicated process of finding a production home was shepherded by my indispensable friend and producing partner Bob Bookman; we've been a tandem for so many years that we've grown old working together. Dana Spector at CAA also shrewdly helped guide me in this process. And both Craig Emanuel and Scott Oranburg at Paul Hastings did all the legal heavy lifting with a careful intelligence. As a result, the book is now being produced as a series by Bri Hennessey and Sherryl Clark for Village Roadshow Productions.

Also, as the pieces came out, I was fortunate to work with and benefit from the knowledge of many media people, including Lisa Soloway, Santina Leuci, Liza Finley, Shane Bishop, Megyn Kelly, Sydney Norton, Bella Lugosi, Peggy Siegal, and Bettina Klinger. And I would be derelict if I didn't mention Kevin Fixler, whose many articles in the *Idaho Statesman* set the authoritative standard for reporting on the continuing events in this case.

And as I hunkered down to write in East Hampton, I was supported throughout the intense process by the kindness and friendship of many, including, in no particular order: Irene and Phil Werber; David and Susan Rich; Sheryl and John Leventhal; Barbara and Ted Ravinett; Sarah and Bill Rauch; Betsey and Len Rappoport; Andrew Solomon and John Habitch; Arlene Mann and Bob Katz; Beth DeWoody; Georgette and Bruce Taub; Kathy Rayner; Bradley Lander; Sara Colleton; Bailey Gimbel; Lori Macgarva; Ken Lipper; Pat Byrne; and Daisy Miller.

And here's as good a place as any for an admission: I owe the inspiration for the title of this book to a haunting song by Bob Dylan, "When the Night Comes Falling from the Sky."

Finally, as in all things in my work and in my life, I am deeply indebted to my sister Marcy and my brother-in-law Destin Coleman. And then there's Ivana, who in her unique way made each day a unique blessing.

NOTE ON SOURCES

As I set out to tell the story of the Idaho murders, I was guided largely by two ambitions. The first was to write the definitive account of the events surrounding the four brutal and confounding homicides. And to accomplish this, I knew I would need to go beyond what had been reported in the media (including the Internet), the statements and documents that had been publicly released by law enforcement, and the court filings of the opposing legal teams. My second aspiration was no less a challenge: I was determined to craft a nonfiction narrative that made the real-life actors come alive to the reader, that was propelled by a frisson of suspense, and, not least, was shaped by the storyteller's art.

Lofty goals, indeed! And, I concede, I faced a fair share of obstacles.

For starters, there was a judicial gag order that, to a significant extent, legally prohibited those who had the most intimate knowledge of events—families of the survivors, law enforcement officials, and attorneys—from speaking directly about what had occurred. Then there was a trial, or, more precisely, its continued postponement. It was originally scheduled for the fall of 2023; as of this writing, a trial date has still not been set, and the prosecution's recent suggestion that the proceedings should commence in the summer of 2025 was, frustratingly, met with dismissive rejoinders from the defense. And without even a viable trial timeline, the much-anticipated courtroom revelations remain dangling beyond any reporter's grasp. Also, perhaps inevitably, as the story dominated the news, show business and book publishers rushed into the fray, too. I, to my delight (and profit), was able to land both a book contract and a series deal. And I was not the only one. There were announcements of other books, other movies, and several documentaries. And since we were getting paid for our labors, people close to the case decided with reason that they had every right to charge for what they had to say, too. I saw their point; it made pragmatic good sense. Yet, for several reasons—paramount among them my training as a *New York Times* reporter—paying for an interview just didn't sit right with me. It felt like a tainted game, and I decided I didn't want to play. And so I was left to forage about without this possible advantage.

Yet despite these hurdles, I did get to the bottom of things. But to tell the previously unreported story in this book, I also had to make some compromises. Out of necessity, many of my sources, particularly those in law enforcement or close to the grand jury who provided the most startling information, insisted that I could not identify them for attribution. I agreed to this request, and I now have no choice but to honor it. Also, several of the key individuals depicted in this account refused to talk to me. For example, I did not interview either Michael Kohberger or Steve Goncalves. Nevertheless, I was able talk at length to people close to them, including relatives, friends, and attorneys. And in addition, there were social media postings, statements to the press, and television and Internet interviews that, when all were collected and reviewed, allowed me to document their thoughts and convictions with a revelatory accuracy. In fact, to locate sources close to many of the individuals I write about with an intimate authority, I took inspiration from the playbook of the prosecution's forensic investigators: I built out a family tree of some of the principals in this tale and then hunted down their relatives—several of whom proved both knowledgeable as well as willing to talk at great length about their relations as long as I promised not to identify them. These sources provided a firsthand insight and awareness into what many of the characters in this book—individuals who refused to speak to me directly—were thinking and feeling.

By the time I started to write, my notebooks and legal pads were filled with the notes from approximately 324 interviews conducted in person and on the phone. This allowed me to write a true story.

Here, then, are the cardinal rules that guided me as I wrote this account: If a statement is in direct quotes, it is information that was conveyed to me in that precise form by an interview, government documents or legal filings, published newspaper articles, books, or a transcript of either a television or Internet interview. And if an incident is depicted, its details were shared directly to me by at least two mutually confirming sources, or a previously published press report or legal filing.

As to my other ambition of trying to craft a suspenseful real-life account, let me share two literary conceits that help me shape the narrative. For one thing, I "borrowed" my structure from Homer. This tale, like *The Odyssey*, employs a road trip, a long journey home, as the story's backbone. And for another, the italicized introductions to each of the sections of this book are literary devices. They are neither direct quotations from any individual nor are they meant to convey the actual thoughts of any individual. Rather, although they appear in a nonfiction book, these italicized sections are fictive constructs, artificial "thought dreams," metaphors for an imagined reality that exists only in my authorial imagination. They are employed to nudge the reader closer to the beating heart of the story. Yet, I also readily concede, the italicized introductions are exceptions to the strict journalistic rules that govern this nonfiction book, which have otherwise been followed doggedly. I will leave it to the reader to decide if this small bit of "playing tennis without a net," as Robert Frost once described free verse, was justified.

Finally, a great deal has been written about this case, and I relied on the work of many diligent and resourceful reporters to flesh out this account. If I were to cite each article I consulted, however, it would require a separate volume. Still, I would be remiss if I didn't cite my reliance on the reporting in the *Idaho Statesman* (Kevin Fixler, who was both perceptive, shrewd, and gracious when I frequently peppered him with questions, as well as Sally Krutzig and Shawn Goodwin) and the *New York Times* (Mike Baker). The Internet, as I detail in the text, also played an important part in advancing the reporting on this case, and when I listened to Jonathan Lee Riches, or Brat Norton, or Olivia Vitale I often learned something new. In addition, cable and YouTube shows such as Brian Entrin on *NewsNation* and the Law and Crime Network were essential viewing. Then, too, there was a daunting collection of public memos and legal documents produced by the Moscow police, the prosecution, and the defense. I made my way through them all, but it would be an unnecessary indulgence (as well as beyond the purpose of this account) to cite them individually.

In the end, this book offers insight and perspective into a breaking news story; it is a largely contemporaneous account of recent events. Therefore, since the occurrences were often widely reported, I am sharing only a very broad description of the many publicly available sources I used; and my attributions are further restricted by the confidentiality agreements I was required to make. A chapter-by-chapter listing follows.

Chapter One: Italicized introduction is a fictive, literary construct. It is an imagined attempt to get inside the mind of an alleged killer, not the suspect's actual thoughts or words; interviews with Michael Kohberger sources [MK Sources]; Kohberger family sources [KS]; press reports [PR]; police documents [PD]; *Moscow-Pullman Daily News* [MPD]; *WSU Insider*; interview with Sheriff Bret Myers [Myers]; federal law enforcement sources [FLE].

Chapter Two: MK Sources; KS; Reddit; Michael Kohberger bankruptcy records; Kohberger family criminal records [KFC]; PR; *Idaho Statesman* [IS]; Pennsylvania interviews [PI]; J. Reuben Appleman, *While Idaho Slept* (New York: Harper, 2023) [Appelman]; Christian Martinez interview [CM].

Chapter Three: CM; Zach Cartwright interview [ZC]; PR; Basseth Salamjohn interview [BS]; MPD; Moscow PD Annual Reports [AR]; Julie R. Monroe, *Moscow: Living and Learning on the Palouse* (Charleston, SC: Arcadia Publishing, 2003); Carol Ryrie Brink, *Buffalo Coat* (Pullman, Washington: Washington State University Press, 1993); Project Safe Childhood, Idaho, source interviews [PSC]; Pastor Doug Wilson interviews [DW]; PR.

Chapter Four: CM; ZC; BS; Party Attendees interviews [PA]; FLE.

Chapter Five: MK Sources; KS; Washington State Criminal Justice Dept Sources [CJS]; Appleman; PR; KFC; DeSales University sources [DS]; Katherine Ramsland, *Inside the Minds of Serial Killers: Why They Kill* (Westport, CT: Praeger, 2006); Ramsland, *Confession of a Serial Killer* (Waltham, MA: ForeEdge, 20016); Reddit.

Chapter Six: MPD; PR; Appleman; DS; CJS; MK Sources; KS; Indiana Law Enforcement Bodycam Videos [IBV].

Chapter Seven: Italicized prologue is a fictive construct, an imagined look into the mind of an alleged killer. It is not an actual quotation from any individual; IBV; Moscow Police Bodycam Video [MBV]; PD; FLE.

Chapter Eight: Interviews with Story Real Estate personnel; Internet Real Estate listing; PR; University of Idaho Student interviews [UIS]; Ashlin Couch family member interview; Appleman.

Chapter Nine: Appleman; PR; Idaho Criminal conviction reports [ICR]; UIS.

Chapter Ten: PR; Appleman; UIS; family of survivors public statements and media interviews [FSI].

Chapter Eleven: UIS; PR; Appleman; FSI.

Chapter Twelve: FSI; UIS; PR; Appleman; MPD; PD; Corner Club sources interviews [CC]; Grub Truck Video [GTV]; FSI; FLE.

Chapter Thirteen: PD; FLE; FSI; PR; Appleman; Legal Filings [LF].

Chapter Fourteen: IBV; MKS; KS; FLE; PD.

Chapter Fifteen: The italicized prologue is a fictive construct. It is an imagined re-creation of the suspect's thoughts. Yet while a fiction, it was informed by conversations with law enforcement and legal sources close to the case and reflects their speculations surrounding an alleged killer's internal ruminations; PD; PR; Moscow Police interviews conducted prior to the gag order [MPDI]; MPD; Whitcom 9-1-1 interviews and press coverage; AR; UIS.

Chapter Sixteen: PD; PR; MPDI; Appleman; FLE; Rand Walker interview [RW].

Chapter Seventeen: PW; PR; MPDI; FLE; PD; LF; Arthur Conan Doyle, *The Adventures of Sherlock Holmes* (Mineola, NY: Dover Books, 2009)[SH].

Chapter Eighteen: FSI; PR; Appleman; PD; text messages sent by Steve Goncalves to associates [SGT]; interviews with Steve Goncalves associates [SGAI]; Olivia Vitale interview [OV].

Chapter Nineteen: OV; Appleman; Sydney Norton interview [SN]; FLE; FSI.

Chapter Twenty: The italicized prologue is a fictive construct. It is not a direct quotation from any individual, but rather an imagined attempt to reconstruct the thoughts of the alleged killer, and it was informed by both law enforcement and legal sources speculations; PD; FLE; MPDI; PR; Appleman; LD; Interviews with Troy Road gas station employees; police videos [PV].

Chapter Twenty-one: FLE; PD; PR; Washington State University police department interviews [WSUPD].

Chapter Twenty-two: PD; PR; Idaho State Forensic Lab personnel interviews [IFL]; Othram laboratory interviews [OL]; FLE; LD.

Chapter Twenty-Three: OL; Charles Johnson interviews; John Burbank interview; FLE; PD; PR; KF; MPDI.

Chapter Twenty-four: FLE; PR; PD; LD; Loma Colorado public records; MK Sources; KF; IBV.

Chapter Twenty-five: FLE; PD; LD; legal defense team sources [LDT]; SH; MK sources; KF; *Dateline* NBC report; PR; Appleman.

Chapter Twenty-six: Pennsylvania state trooper interviews [PST]; Pennsylvania associates of troopers interviews [PSTA]; FLE; PR; PD; LD; OL.

Chapter Twenty-seven: PST; PSTA; PR; FLE; interviews with Indian Mountain Lakes residents.

Chapter Twenty-eight: Jason LaBar interviews [JLB]; PR; Appleman; Monroe County Jail interviews; LaBar public statements [JLBS]; PV; Moscow police press conference; MK sources; KF; DS.

Chapter Twenty-nine: The italicized prologue is a fictive construct. It is an imagined attempt to get into the minds of members of the defense team and does not purport to be a direct quotation of statements made by them; LDT; PD; MPD; LD; Appleman; PR; Reddit; MPDI; FLE.

Chapter Thirty: LDT; FLE; PD; OL; SGAI; SGT; LD.

Chapter Thirty-one: PR; Idaho and Washington State criminal records; Caden Young death investigation, including interviews with detectives, recordings made by police with principals, and interview with legal aid attorney [CYDI]; Christopher O'Flaherty interviews [COF]; PR; Emma Bailey DUI video; police recording of Kimberley Bailey interview; UIS; Washington State University student interviews; Tanner Aspire interview.

Chapter Thirty-two: LDT; Seattle DEA interview: Myers; UIS; Couch family interview; PR; FLE; ZC; BS; CM; PA; DW.

Chapter Thirty-three: The italicized prologue is a fictive construct. It is not a direct quotation from Steve Goncalves, nor is it a direct quotation made by any family member whose child was killed in the house on King Road. Rather, guided by the public statements made by the parents whose children were murdered on November 13, it is an attempt to shape a fictive parent's thoughts and emotions; SGAI; SGT; PR; Appleman; OV; FLE; PD; LD.

Epilogue: The italicized prologue is a fictive construct. It is an imagined and empathetic look into the minds and hearts of those who were close to the four murdered students; PD; PR; the author's musings on how a killer finds the will to act were initially inspired (albeit broadly) by John le Carré's explanation of the internal forces that cause an individual to become a traitor, as put forth in *The Secret Pilgrim*.

224

ABOUT THE AUTHOR

HOWARD BLUM is the author of the *New York Times* bestseller and Edgar Award winner for the true crime book *American Lightning*, as well as several other nonfiction bestsellers. His articles on the Idaho murders in *Air Mail* were nominated for the Pulitzer Prize for feature writing, and were featured on many television shows and podcasts, including *48 Hours*, *20/20*, and *The Megyn Kelly Show*. While at the *New York Times*, he was twice nominated for a Pulitzer Prize for investigative reporting. He is the father of three grown children and lives in Connecticut and East Hampton.